CROSSING BORDERS

Reframing undocumented immigration into the United States

Pedro J. Lopes

ALEXANDRIA LIBRARY
PUBLISHING HOUSE
MIAMI

A José Páramo y a Guillermo Álvarez,
maestros de mi "escolaridad" elemental.

A todas as mulheres da minha vida
(elas sabem quem são).

To all of those
whose hearts beat like ours.

Dos horas después el corazón de fray Bartolomé Arrazola chorreaba su sangre vehemente sobre la piedra de los sacrificios (brillante bajo la opaca luz de un sol eclipsado), mientras uno de los indígenas recitaba sin ninguna inflexión de voz, sin prisa, una por una, las infinitas fechas en que se producirían eclipses solares y lunares, que los astrónomos de la comunidad maya habían previsto y anotado en sus códices sin la valiosa ayuda de Aristóteles.

Augusto Monterroso
"El Eclipse"

Por el camino hasta perdimos el derecho de llamarnos americanos, aunque los haitianos y los cubanos ya habían asomado a la historia, como pueblos nuevos, un siglo antes de que los peregrinos del Mayflower se establecieran en las costas de Plymouth. Ahora América es, para el resto del mundo, nada más que los Estados Unidos: nosotros habitamos, a lo sumo, una sub América, una América de segunda clase, de nebulosa identificación.

Eduardo Galeano
Las Venas Abiertas de América Latina

Man hat Arbeitskräfte gerufen, und es kommen Menschen.

Max Frisch

Table of Contents

Foreword

Mike Young , MA
Director of Capacity Building at PASOs

Bella Rosa Guardado fled El Salvador for the promise of a better life in the United States the day after Mother's Day in 1973 at the age of eighteen. Making it to the Mexican border town of Tijuana with her brother and one of her uncles, there was a major hiccup. The coyotes had trained them for what to do if they got caught, and they did. She buried all her paperwork, passport, and identification in the California sand just before she was hauled back to Mexico. She did as she was instructed and said she was Mexican from the Yucatan peninsula area (explaining why she spoke a different breed of Spanish); her brother and uncle weren't as convincing and were deported back to El Salvador. Alone in Tijuana with only $50 to her name, Bella spent two weeks in a $5-a-night hotel befriending any kindhearted person she met while avoiding the predators that lurked and preyed on young women like her.

After running out of money, she slept in the hotel office, generous lodging offered by the sympathetic manager. Many people came through this hotel and offered to help once she got into the United States. These phone numbers and promises were the only things that kept her hopes alive. Agreeing to work with Don Ramon, a fledgling

11

and seemingly trustworthy coyote, she spent four grueling days attempting to get to the other side of the border. In one day, she was caught five times. Malnourishment left her weighing a frail eighty-three pounds when she finally made it to meet her contact- her third attempt that day.

Not knowing a word of English, she was completely dependent on her coyote host who allowed her to stay with his family until she could find a way to repay her debt for the crossing: $275. Crammed in a two-bedroom house with Don Ramon, his wife and their six children, Bella called the contact she made while at the Tijuana hotel, a Guatemalan family living in the San Fernando Valley. Making good on their promise to help, they contacted help wanted ads on her behalf and that same weekend she landed her first job making $35 a week as a live-in housekeeper/babysitter for Fred and Sara Lee Young and their two sons.

Six months into the job, the couple had marital problems and he left the house; they later divorced.. Four months after that, Bella was unhappy with the work situation and found another job with a different family, but still kept in contact with the man of the house. Fred and Bella married in 1977.

Fred came into some money from his life insurance and decided to invest in the Mexican banking system that was offering 32% interest for large deposits that are left untouched for two years. Sadly, in 1982, the Mexican economy crashed and the devaluing of the peso devastated his savings. An acquaintance in Mexico offered Fred and Bella beachfront Mexican property in exchange for the savings. They decided to make the switch, but the Mexican constitution forbade foreigners owning Mexican soil, especially beachfront property. Bella happened to be pregnant with her second child during all of this and they decided that if the baby was born in Mexico, he or she would automatically be a Mexican citizen and able to own land.

I know this story intimately because Bella Rosa is my mother and I am proud to say that at the time of my birth, I was a landowning Mexican citizen born to an American and an El Salvadoran migrant who struggled to escape Mexico, only to have her second child be born an hour south of where it might have all ended.

The following pages demonstrate Pedro Lopes' mastery of Latin American history related to the implications of global forces that influence the incredible odds individuals grapple with when they decide to migrate. Lopes' comprehensive approach highlights trends and disparities across periods of time and generational decision-making at different stages within each of their respective lives, all situated within specific national contexts. What I hope to contribute is a face, a name, a noticeably vibrant single thread in the tapestry that makes up the fabric of our current United States.

My mother doesn't look back on her heroic journey as something she was escaping. She saw a bright future— one that wasn't possible if she remained where she was. Having only attained a sixth grade education while living without running water or electricity most of her life, she couldn't understand why her circumstances were lopsided. This book helps provide a greater context as to why the many Bella Rosas throughout Latin America born in different decades continue to search for a better life. . In order for us to understand their story, we must see their humanity. We must hear their names and listen to their stories. That is the only way we will be able to authentically generate empathy, which then needs to be matched with action. My mother's story influenced me to question reality, ultimately to study cultural anthropology, and work toward a doctorate in that field. I am now a director for PASOs , which means "steps" in Spanish, the largest statewide organization that advocates for and supports the Latino population of South Carolina, documented or not. We see the potential in others; we nurture their strengths.

My mother received citizenship during President Ronald Reagan's Amnesty of 1986 and is now a computer component engineer and works for one of the leading medical device manufacturers that produces lifesaving machines within hospitals. Her story and the foundation it laid for my own is a mixture of luck, mistakes, successes, failures, devastations, and triumphs. Her journey could have gone down many different avenues and we know that many others are at different stages within similar stories. We must recognize their struggles, and in true Freirean solidarity, take action to assist.

The following poem follows my mother's path and diverges into alternative potential possibilities that may not have happened, but could have.

Chase the Sun

Barshigaye Behek[1]

I.

Mama, I'm leaving now

The train is calling me

I'm following my dreams of a better life for all of us

I promise I'll send money every third Tuesday on the dot

They pay by the hour there

Don't worry mama I'll come back for you

While I'm gone when you look up at the night sky and see the stars

Know that I'm thinking of you

But for now I'm off to chase the sun

II.

I'm so close I can taste it

My knuckles dig into the dirt below me

Dragged by my ankles thrown into a van

I sleep on concrete

Spend weeks in a motel manager's back room

People watch me

People judge me

They make promises to help me

1. Q'eqchi' Maya words for "where are you going" response: "to wander," a common phrase exchanged between individuals.

I cross the line
They crossed the line
Into the desert I find my way
Carrying gallons of water on my back
Through barren wasteland
Mouth parched by heat
I'm being chased by the sun

To the horizon
I claw

Pray for rain

Now I only get to watch the sun set behind tall buildings
Behind tall buildings

III.

I don't believe the lies
That I was told when I was young
This isn't paradise
Land of sacrifice
I want to take it back
I don't remember the last time I looked into my mother's eyes
Or held my brother's hand
I traded my innocence and childhood
For a clock that never stops, never gets tired
But I do
At night I'm afraid of what might happen to me
I hardly ever see the sun these days

We chase the sun
And I claw

Preface

The complexity surrounding undocumented immigration in the United States is often oversimplified in public discourse as to engender a narrative dichotomized between the plain notions of legal and illegal. Added to the generally fallacious characterization of its effects on the economy and on society at large, undocumented immigration is thus seldom properly contextualized. The disregard for the historical roots of the problem, as well as for the inner workings of the due process of legalization, have become the bedrock of deceiving and often absurd accounts on the subject. Furthermore, this historical perspective is aggravated by the perpetuation of a naïve sentiment of moral authority underlying the application of the rule of law to differentiate between citizens and aliens, a mechanism that serves well some political agendas.

Under this shroud of ignorance, naiveté, and deception lies a reality that runs deeper than the assumptions permeating the collective imagination of the country and woven into the fabric of its political and legal systems.

In *Crossing Borders* I scrutinize the historical foundations of undocumented immigration into the United States, as well as the most consequential legislation adopted over the years to justify a record of, arguably, selective legality. By offering to give a voice to a few of those who actually engaged in the perilous undertaking of traversing borders clandestinely, I hope to foil the process of dehumanization of these individuals that percolates the language of the main-stream media and informs the dominant political discourse.

According to Migrants Rights International citing UN estimates, more than 200 million people live outside their country of birth, either permanently or temporarily, legally or otherwise.[2] Before delving into the reasons why, in the particular case of Mexico and Central America, it is important to note that few of them leave their homelands driven by greed, and even fewer out of sheer boredom. If we consider the importance given to family in these Latin-based cultures, then it becomes apparent that leaving loved ones behind must not be an easy decision; it also suggests the existence of compelling and force majeure factors pressing migrants to abandon their roots. This is a socio-economic reality one must acknowledge and in all its facets. We must also come to grips with the paradox behind the fact that those claiming to be legal citizens, mostly of European descent, have their prerogative less justified by ancestry than those *aliens* they are trying to exclude, many of whom trace their lineage back to pre-Columbian times. Even if we dismiss this oddity as an anecdotal relic of history and anachronous vis-à-vis modern political boundaries, we must nevertheless acknowledge the pivotal role of American foreign policy itself in precipitating a massive displacement of people originating south of its borders. Concurrently, and just as importantly, is the fact that the relationship between U.S. development and immigration, especially from Mexico beginning in the 19th century, has been one of symbiosis and dependence. As such, the level of tolerance to immigrants and of the permissiveness of immigration fluctuated according to economic cycles and the shifting needs of the American labor market. By 1924 Mexicans

---

2. "MRI's Origins." Migrants Rights International, MRI, (n/d), migrantsrightsinternational.org/mri-origins (accessed January 17, 2019).

were considered "white" in the United States, and therefore gained exemption from the immigrant exclusion act of that year— no doubt owing it to the pressures of labor interests north of the border. Accordingly, Aristide Zolberg observes that immigration policy in 19th century U.S. "involved from the outset a combination of disparate elements designed to facilitate or even stimulate the entry of immigrants deemed valuable."[3] The same author remarks that such policy was also and simultaneously aimed at "deterring those considered undesirable, and occasionally even going beyond this to rid the nation of populations already in its midst." The expression "undesirable aliens," mentioned in the 1922 Annual Report of the Commissioner General of Immigration to the Secretary of Labor, certainly encapsulates the capriciousness nature of the criteria underlying the distinction between who was to be welcomed and who was to be refused legal admittance in the country.

But the role of corporate interests does not end here. The United States, as a major exponent of global capitalism, has long been a paragon of an economic doctrine where "people are displaced because the economies of their countries of origin are transformed, to enable corporations and national elites to transfer wealth out."[4] This is arguably the strongest justification for the aforementioned American foreign policy, which, regardless of its misleading pretenses, has aimed at preserving colonial ownership structures thereby curtailing any signs of developmentalism and stopping on its tracks any discordant revisions to the free-market orthodoxy.[5] Most Central

---

3. Zolberg, Aristide R. A Nation by Design: Immigration Policy in the Fashioning of America. Cambridge, MA: Harvard University Press, 2006, 19.

4. Bacon, David. Illegal People: How Globalization Creates Migration and Criminalizes Immigrants. Beacon Press, 2008, 69.

5. Developmentalism is an approach to the economy whereby the development of less-than-industrialized nations rests upon the cultivation of a strong and diverse internal market and on limiting the countries' dependence on the

American countries know this reality well, as demonstrated by the fact that there was no substantial migration out of Central America until the 1980s, when the grip of the U.S. military-based state corporatism was tightest in its zealous defense of what was to be more brazenly called "American interests" in the region.[6]

Equally relevant to the exploration of the matter in hand is sketching a profile of who these "aliens" are. Historically, Mexicans have comprised the bulk of both immigration into the Unites States at large (superseded only by the Europeans welcomed at Ellis Island), as well as that achieved by clandestine means.[7] They are also the majority among those traversing the border surreptitiously, estimating by the number of apprehensions at the border. These numbers are likely somewhat swollen by Central Americans who, for their own protection, try not to stand out as non-Mexican, often even concealing the fact from authorities and other migrants, so that as to avoid deportation all the way back to isthmus from which a crossing retrial is increasingly onerous. For this reason, the label "Mexicans" was routinely generically attached to individuals of other nationalities

---

exports of raw resources by fostering the growth of national industries. High tariffs on imported goods is another hallmark of this doctrine based on the import-substitution development model.

6. In an interview to The Guardian regarding his book, the former CIA agent Philip Agee summarizes the years leading up to the surge in north-bound migration originating in Central America as a time "when the worst imaginable horrors were going on in Latin America. Argentina, Brazil, Chile, Uruguay, Paraguay, Guatemala, El Salvador - they were military dictatorships with death squads, all with the backing of the CIA and the US government" (Campbell, Duncan. "Philip Agee: The man who blew the whistle on the CIA's backing of military dictatorships." The Guardian. Guardian News & Media Limited, 10 January 2008, theguardian.com/news/2008/jan/10/mainsection.duncancampbell. Accessed February 5, 2019).

7. As of 2015, the number of illegal immigrants residing in the United States is estimated at 12 million, 60% of whom from Mexico.

the border authorities were unable of, or uninterested in distinguishing at the time. Even today, the expression OTM ("Other Than Mexican") is used, which is telling of the prevalence of Mexican nationals among all clandestine crossers— about 93% by the beginning of the present decade.[8]

Subsequently, and in concert with geographical proximity, the social capital accrued by Mexican nationals expanded in direct proportion to the ever larger swaths of migrants originating in all regions of Mexico. This sociologic phenomenon is intrinsic to the consolidation of the social networks (formed by family members, friends, neighbors, etc.) that facilitate further migration— a process we may call autocatalytic.[9]

In the meantime, the fable of legal immigration as an option permeates the collective imagination to a considerable extent, similar to the myth that Republican administrations in Washington are "tougher" on illegal immigration, when facts point to the contrary.[10] Waiting times for immigrant visas run in the decades (!), while the ideological disposition to regard "amnesty" as liberalist continuously undermines any prospects of legalization for currently undocumented immigrants in the country. These considerations are irrespective of our reckoning the generic benefits of immigration, which falls outside the scope of the present text.

All things considered, a world where globalization implies free transit of capital and goods, but, alas, not of people, inevitably fuels fear-mongering and wall-building hysteria, on the heels of the not less inevitable displacement it generates. It is thus imperative to

8. Henderson, Timothy J. Beyond Borders: A History of Mexican Migration to the United States. Malden, MA: Wiley-Blackwell, 2011, 1.

9. Spener, David. Clandestine Crossings: Migrants and Coyotes on the Texas-Mexico Border. Ithaca: Cornell UP, 2009, 112.

10. For example, during the Obama administration the number of deportations reached an all-time record.

abandon at once the pretense that illegal immigration is a problem exogenous to the economic system we so enthusiastically embrace. Only then will we be in position to analyze it not exclusively as a political, economic, and social concern, but also one of harrowing humanitarian consequences.

It is not my intention herein to make an apologetic defense of immigration, legal or otherwise, on either ethical or pragmatic grounds. I merely propose a foundation on which to base a sounder debate of these matters, one informed with the proper historical framework and aware of some of the legal and procedural realities faced by those who resort to leave their countries of birth behind. Once on the subject, we will learn of the risks and difficulties involved in such enterprise.

Terminology

Given the wide range of expressions that characterize the discussion pertaining to the movement of individuals across borders, much confusion surrounds certain concepts associated with the non-native-born at large. For example, it is baffling how the word *citizenship* is so often carelessly and spuriously employed in public discourse. This confusion is perpetuated by sophistic political rhetoric, generally more aimed at indoctrinating than at elucidating; and by inadequate media coverage of the subject, thus making it typical among those less familiarized with it. Whether some of this lexicon is used in the text below or not, it is nevertheless important to deconstruct the implications of word choice in understanding what is at stake. Additionally, the clarification may also aid to demystify certain misconstructions associated with the issue of immigration in general.

Migration is generally accepted to mean the generic movement of people or animals from one region to another. When applied to humans, this movement tends to be for economic or political reasons and is often temporary. **Immigration**, on the other hand, implies that this relocation is made by crossing political or physical borders into a third country with a firmer purpose of permanent settling there. In the present text, the choice of vocabulary between the two concepts is processed as rigorously as possible as to reflect different cases and circumstances, although it is not always possible to determine, often by the (im)migrants themselves, the intended length of stay in unfamiliar lands— even assuming their plans do not change over time. **Emigration** refers to a notion similar to immigration, with the difference being the point of view, as it refers to those individuals leaving their country to settle elsewhere. In this work, and for the sake of consistency, a conscientious effort is made to employ, whenever possible, the word *migrants* to refer to individuals in the process of migrating, and *immigrants* when their presence in the host country is more of less permanent. **Remigration** denotes the return back to country of origin on the part of those who had previously migrated abroad.

Illegal immigration is when the entry and long-term settlement of individuals in another country is carried out without the proper legal documentation required by the host nation. In the United States, those individuals found in such circumstances are interchangeably labeled *illegal immigrants, undocumented immigrants,* or *illegal aliens.* Although the semantics of these designations renders dehumanizing effects of varying degrees on the subjects they describe, different statuses attributed to non-natural-born citizens in the United States actually recommend a more conscientious choice of words, corresponding to differentiated legal predicaments. Equally relevant is the distinction between different shades of illegality under the law, lest we forget illegal entry in the country is simply a misdemeanor, and only its recurrence is considered a felony.[11]

A **passport** is a travel document issued by one's country of citizenship and may be obtained, in most cases, by anyone who applies for one with the respective authorities of each nation, provided that no criminal charges or other disputes impede such issuance

---

11. Guskin, Jane, and David L. Wilson. The Politics of Immigration: Questions and Answers. New York: Monthly Review, 2007, 41.

and consequent authorization to leave the country is granted. This process generally requires payment and proof of citizenship and guarantees the return of the passport holder to his or her country of citizenship after travelling abroad. A **visa**, on the other hand, is an endorsement issued on a passport by the authorities of a foreign country allowing its holder to enter such nation. Visas usually either specify the length of stay during which the visitor is allowed to remain within its borders; or the period of time during which (repeated) admittance will be granted. It is important to keep in mind that a visa is not *necessarily* equivalent to a working permit, nor does it authorize permanent residency in a country. In the case of the United States, the Department of State issues a myriad of different types of visas, from tourist visas to student visas (under the broad category of *nonimmigrant* visas), and seemingly everything else in between, including some worker visa categories that have in common the fact of being *temporary* in scope. Be that as it may, neither a foreign passport nor a visa are ever guarantees of granted entry of their respective holders in the United States.

A **green card**[12] is associated with the status of permanent residency granted to foreign nationals in the United States. The status of Permanent Resident allows foreign nationals to live and work in the United States— but it does not confer upon them the right to vote or hold federal elective office. The process of obtaining a permanent resident card is usually preceded by the issuance of a *work permit*, which the eventual granting of a green card revokes and replaces. Permanent resident cards expire and must be renewed typically in 10-year cycles.

---

12. The design and color of the Permanent Resident card has evolved over the decades, but it has retained its name from the color of the original document. It has also held its official designation as Form I-551 since after World War II.

Naturalization is the granting of full-rights, citizenship status and rights thereof of a natural-born citizen to foreign-born nationals. To qualify for naturalization in the United States, among other eligibility requirements, prospective citizens must hold the status of permanent residents (i.e., held a green card) for a minimum of five years— or three if married to a U.S. citizen. The naturalization process includes, but is not limited to, passing an English and civics test as well as renouncing previous citizenship and allegiance to country of origin.[13] In the United States as in most other nations, the eligibility for holding the office of president or vice-president of the country is a prerogative of natural-born citizens only and is therefore unattainable for naturalized citizens.

Deportation (or **removal**) is the act of apprehending and transporting undocumented immigrants back to their country of origin by immigration authorities. In the United States, the entities responsible for immigration affairs and the enforcement of immigration laws are currently under the broader administrative realm of the Department of Homeland Security (DHS). Formerly known as Immigration and Naturalization Services, three different branches were created in 2003 to replace the INS, and its functions were subsequently transferred to the USCIS (United States Citizenship and Immigration Services), the ICE (Immigration and Customs Enforcement), and the CBP (Customs and Border Protection). **Repatriation** is another term sometimes used as a synonym, albeit with a distinctive, less menacing semantic charge, but all referring to the same process of expulsion on non-nationals.

---

13. Laws concerning dual-citizenship or dual-nationality status are complex and vary from country to country. In the United States, immigration laws are generally omissive in this regard. The policy towards non natural-born citizens holding dual-citizenship status seems to be one of discouraging rather than proscribing.

Push and Pull factors are the circumstances that encourage the displacement of people who opt to settle in a region other than that of their origin. When unfavorable political or economic conditions at the origin force the departure of individuals and families in search of better opportunities elsewhere, they are called *push factors;* when the primary forces behind the relocation to another region or country are the allure of life enhancement at the destination, they are called *pull factors.* The distinction is academic, insofar as in practice, both types of factors contribute most often in conjunction to complex migratory fluxes across borders.

A **coyote** (from the Nāhuatl *coyōtl*) is a common denomination attributed to those individuals who engage in the practice (i.e., *coyotage*) of facilitating clandestine human traffic northbound across the U.S.-Mexican border. The figure of the coyote has been prevalent in Mexican cosmology and folklore since ancient times, due to the canid's proven resourcefulness to negotiate complicated situations and thus overcoming more powerful opponents. Predating illegal border-crossing, the metaphor served to label any person who made a living out of cunningly circumventing bureaucratic hurdles of various kinds on behalf of paying third parties.[14] This role of intermediary is not only fitting in the context of undocumented border-crossing, where the coyote supplies the crossing strategies that best guard from detection and safety risks; it is also suited to their function of middlemen between prospective undocumented workers and employers across the border.[15] Finally, the empirical association

---

14. The need to bypass bureaucratic procedures is justified in societies in which rules and regulations place an unreasonable burden on those without access to privileged channels of expediency and who therefore encounter considerable obstacles in their access to even some basic services.

15. As we will see below, the primary role of coyotes in periods of labor shortage and lax, or even nonexistent, border control in the second half of the nineteenth and into the first half of the twentieth centuries was precisely that—

between coyotes and chickens (*pollos*, in Spanish), where the former strive to evade the scrutinizing gaze of farmers to gain access to the latter, has also earned them the label **pollero**. **Patero** (related to the crossing on shallow-draught boats called *patos* in Spanish, or "ducks") is another colloquial designation for these individuals, albeit the use of these last two terms is not as geographically widespread and common as the more generic "*coyote*." Today, the role of a coyote may also imply the negotiation of various logistical aspects associated with guarding and conducting their costumers to safety in their final destinations in the United States, generally working in concert with a network of other coyotes.[16]

Wetback is a derogatory term referring to illegal immigrants, specifically those crossing the southern border clandestinely. The origin of the ethnically charged label constitutes an allusion to the first years of surreptitious border crossing, namely due to the fact that most unauthorized entries into the United States implied crossing, often by swimming it, the river lying at the intersection of the two countries— the Rio Grande, or Río Bravo (del Norte), as it is known in Mexico. The sense of wetness caused by the journey across the banks of the river forming a natural border between Texas and Mexico is also conveyed in the Spanish equivalent: **mojado,** or simply "wet." In like manner, the term **alambrista** (derived from *alambre*, or "wire", in Spanish) is sometimes used to differentiate those who, instead, make the cross through gaps in the border fencing. In Spanish border-crossing jargon, the word **pollos** ("chickens") is also widely used, not to refer to undocumented immigrants already residing in the United States, but rather to those in the actual process

---

recruiting and transporting workers from south of the border on behalf of eager American landowners and other employing entities in various fields of economic activity.

16. Spener 94.

of crossing the border stealthily. The origin of the moniker, which naturally relates to the term *pollero* mentioned above, is obscure and may draw different connections. One is a sense of defenselessness of these travelers at the hands of often less than scrupulous coyotes. Another connotation hints at the commanding sounds produced by *crossing guides* during the journey to hens in distress. Finally, it may also metaphorically allude to the image of vulnerable chicks trustfully following their mother hen to safety.

Bracero is a word derived from the Spanish *brazo*, or "arm," used to describe Mexican migrant workers who participated in the Bracero Program labor arrangement, in effect in the United States between 1942 and 1964. The root of the moniker highlights the unskilled, manual labor these migrants were contracted to perform, mostly in agriculture during times dictated by seasonal demand.

Asylum is the status granted by nations to foreign citizens who are regarded as being victims of prosecution in their own country on the basis of religion, race, nationality, political affiliation, family relationships, or social connections. The granting of asylum is restricted to those individuals meeting the strict definition of **refugee**, which the United States establishes as citizens displaced from their country of origin who fear their return home will seriously threaten their physical integrity. The term **exile** is used when a status associated with "humanitarian" concerns is applied to heads of state who, after being forcefully ousted from power, find their presence in the territory rejected by their countrymen and therefore resort to fleeing to a friendly nation. It is important to note that the terms *asylum* and *exile* are often confused and even used interchangeably, less due to technicalities than to political agility. This confusion is flagrant, for example, in the discourse surrounding the issue of Cuban nationals seeking sanctuary in the United States since the 1960s until recently. Due to the particular set of political circumstances involving the

United States and Cuba, successive American administrations have held a rather permissive and altruistic approach to Cuban citizens who managed to reach American shores upon fleeing the island. This generated a large community of Cuban expatriates residing in the United States who are designated either as "exiles," "refugees," or even, although less commonly, "asylees." The United States Citizenship and Immigration Services (USCIS) currently allows the pursuit of work permits, and eventually permanent residency and citizenship, to asylees and refugees under certain conditions and within a defined timeline, although its scope has tended to narrow over time.

Latino and *Hispanic* are terms used widely and mostly interchangeably in the United States to refer to Spanish-speaking individuals who originate in Latin America or the Caribbean. These terms draw upon the European cultural and linguistic heritage of most Latin American and Caribbean nations, namely via their association with the Latin peoples of Europe, heirs of the Roman Empire, and specifically its Hispania region, modernly comprised of Spain and Portugal. Such nomenclatures fall short, however, of accommodating the native peoples of those regions whose ancestry predates the Spanish conquest. While many individuals of Mayan descent, for instance, identify mainly with the prevalent Latin-based culture of their native countries, it is not uncommon to find families and communities who relate to their indigenous roots to a much larger extent, some of whom do not even speak Spanish at all. On the other hand, the case of Brazil renders the labeling even more questionable, since Brazilians, for the most part, tend to resist being classified under either term— as do Portuguese and Spanish nationals, for that matter. On these grounds, the mention of country of origin or nationality whenever possible is thus preferable when referring to these *Americans*.

Nativists are individuals whose political views are characterized by the will to preserve their indigenous culture. In the case of the United States, the term carries blatant incongruity, inasmuch as its association with an anti-immigrant stance crassly overlooks the demographic and political circumstances at the foundation of the nation. The term is often interlaced with that referring to *Restrictionists*, whose main political agenda seeks to impose restrictions to immigration into the country, both legal and illegal.

Remittances are the monies foreign workers send home to their countries of origin. These financial transfers have become so important to certain developing nations as to represent major sources of foreign currency, even surpassing the revenue generated by large sectors of their own economies.

Part 1
Historical Context

Providing a backdrop for any issue is fundamental to contextualize the contention that may arise from it, as well as to shed light on the possible paths for its solution. As with any historical framework, there are obvious risks associated with delving into the roots of illegal immigration into the United States. For one, because the examination of the past relies on narratives, history is not an objective account of chronologically tabulated events; it is rather a subjective rendition and reconstruction of the past, and therefore a subsidiary interpretation of the cause and effect links connecting events and circumstances over hundreds of years. Secondly, we are posed with the systemic dilemma of how far back to go in order to obtain a satisfactory historical foundation to the realities we aim at examining.

It is equally relevant to consider the natural association between illegal immigration and immigration at large, especially in a country like the United States, where it is commonplace to refer to its ethnic, social, political, and economic makeup as a result of a melting pot of cultures and nationalities that informs its identity as a "nation of immigrants." But the process of different peoples coming together contributing to the current demographic anatomy of the country has not always been peaceful and without struggle. It is thus imperative to outline the historical framework of overall immigration fluxes into the United States as a basis to more appropriately isolate the phenomenon of unauthorized immigration, which is of particular interest herein.

Not being, or claiming to be, an historian by education nor training, I relied heavily on the assistance of others in guiding me, either as primary or secondary sources, through the intricacies of historical fact and record, as well as in navigating the meanders of the legislative landscape framing undocumented immigration. All noted sources have proven to be invaluable, although I feel particularly and especially indebted to a few authors whose meticulous works lay at the foundation of my own.

In no particular order, Mark Reisler's *By the Sweat of Their Brow* provides a unique account, if not one of the first, of the dynamics of Mexican immigrant labor in the United States during the first half of the 20th century, which in turn imparts a sharp perspective on the connection between economic development and migration, with its obvious ties to that of undocumented status.

In parallel, Timothy Henderson delves into the socioeconomic and political dynamics at the base of such migration fluxes in his remarkable *Beyond Borders: A History of Mexican Migration to the United States*. By examining the history of northbound Mexican migration, the author imparts a thorough understanding of both push and pull factors underlying the migratory trends from Mexico to the United States over different eras.

In *Globalization & Migration*, Eliot Dickinson meticulously explores the global context in which the displacement of millions of human beings occurs, demonstrating how the expansion of market-driven societies actually depends on it. In the process, Dickinson draws the connections between such capitalist impulses and the migration fluxes they generate, including in the particular case of Mexico and Central America.

Patrick Ettinger's superb *Imaginary Lines* provided a perspective on the relations of reciprocity between not only labor demands and migration lures, but also on the role of immigration control and enforcement over the decades in regulating the fluidity of the latter in tune with the latent interests of the former. Complementing this analysis is the also excellent *Clandestine Crossings*, where David Spener offers a rendition on the actual processes of surreptitious border crossing, which is validated by the interviews I conducted myself and are part of this text.

Finally, I relied on Daniel Kanstroom's sterling works to help portray the harsh reality of immigration law, particularly incarceration and deportation of undocumented foreign nationals. Although extraneous to undocumented crossings per se, these issues relate aptly to the various means utilized to enter the country illicitly. Even more pertinently, they are also connected with the repeated attempts at doing so, and therefore shed light on the aggravated legal predicaments faced by recurrent offenders and the more-than-likely removal proceedings resulting thereof.

To these scholars their due credit.

U.S. Origins

Considering the inexistence of established political borders at the time, the disembarking of the first Europeans on American soil in the 1500s can hardly be called "immigration," since national borders had not yet been established. More accurately, the great numbers of Old World colonial settlers constituted a massive migration as the result of conditions both at origin, first, and then at destination, that encouraged and facilitated such human displacement.

Less than two decades into the creation of the new nation, the first U.S. census, completed in 1790, puts at 5 million the number of residents in the territory born elsewhere, even though a "question on place of birth, which is the primary source of data on the foreign-born population, was not added until the 1850 census."[17] After that, about 32 million European immigrants arrived in the United States in the period of 1820-1932, comprising the bulk of new residents in the country.[18] As for motivating factors, there seems to be little variation across the different groups, ranging from unfavorable religious, economic, and/or political conditions at the origin (the *push* factors) to the demand of an increased workforce to sustain the

17. Bohme, Frederick G. et al. 1973. Population and Housing Inquiries in U.S. Decennial Censuses, 1790-1970. U.S. Bureau of the Census, Working Paper No. 39. Washington DC: U.S. Government Printing Office.
18. Bailey, Rayna. Immigration and Migration. New York: Facts On File, 2008.

needs of the ongoing industrialization process in the U.S. (the *pull* factors).

This phenomenon is not, in nature, different from the migratory trends that brought the pre-Columbian peoples of North America to the continent from Asia thousands of years before the first Europeans set foot in America. It nevertheless represents the first clash of cultures to take place in the New World, that between newcomers and the indigenous population.

U.S. and Mexico

In the particular case of the United States and Mexico, the porosity of the frontier to the flow of people and culture (and hence to a substantial northbound Hispanic cultural heritage that explains, and historically legitimizes, its demographics), has its roots not only in the ancestral circulation of migrants but also in the shifting of the border itself. Before the conflict known as the Mexican-American War (1846-48), the territories corresponding to the modern American states of California, Nevada, and Utah, as well as to large portions of the current states of New Mexico, Arizona, Colorado, and Wyoming, were part of Mexico. In the aftermath of the conflict, the Treaty of Guadalupe Hidalgo established, among other provisions, that Mexico relinquish what represented about 55% of its pre-war landmass by transferring to the United States its territories north of Rio Grande, known in Mexico as *Río Bravo del Norte*.[19] The annexation of these lands implied, at least on paper, the guarantee of preservation of rights to private ownership of land to the citizens who occupied these areas. Consequently, the United States also "inherited" a large percentage of Mexicans who chose to remain in the newly

---

19. "The Treaty of Guadalupe Hidalgo." National Archives. The U.S. National Archives and Records Administration, (n/d.), archives.gov/education/lessons/guadalupe-hidalgo (accessed October 25, 2016).

acquired domains, albeit under a new flag, and who automatically received American citizenship status in the process. It is estimated at between 80,000 and 100,000 the number of Mexicans who opted to remain in the United States under these circumstances after 1848.[20]

In addition to the cultural and topographic affinities between the borderlands of the U.S. and Mexico, and despite the newly-created division separating the two nations, economic conditions determined that northbound migrant fluxes would remain residual until the end of the century. If anything, there was a more significant migratory wave towards the south, mostly comprised of those Mexican citizens who opted out of the new geography and left the annexed territories to resettle in the much-reduced version of Mexico. For the same reasons, the issue of clandestine border-crossing holds little validity in this context. In the particular case of the Texas-Mexican border, the dislocation of the national political boundaries to the south had little impact on the social, cultural, and even economic praxis of the population, given the strong cultural ties that insisted on bonding the banks across the Río Bravo. Américo Paredes mentions the flow of "farm products from Mexico to Texas, textiles and other manufactured goods from Texas to Mexico" as a clear sign that custom and tradition prevailed over the letter of the law in the first few decades of the new border. Moreover, Paredes points out that "unofficial crossings also disregarded immigration laws," further exemplifying that "children born on one side of the river would be baptized on the other side, and thus appear on church registers as citizens of the other country."[21] Coerver and Hall corroborate this idea when pointing out that "inhabitants of the region viewed the

---

20. Henderson 9.

21. Paredes, Américo, and Richard Bauman. Folklore and Culture on the Texas-Mexican Border. Austin, TX: CMAS, Center for Mexican American Studies, U of Texas at Austin, 1993, 26.

Rio Grande as a connecting force rather than a line of division."[22] These acts of smuggling and clandestine border transit, as described in merely legal terms, are therefore indicative of the broader philosophical implications that, by any reasonable standard, confer a degree of cultural legitimacy to the fluidity of people and goods across the border. What's more, this socioeconomic promiscuity renders the whole issue of illegal immigration from Mexico into the United States as historically problematic. On the other hand, the prevalence of the nuances depicted supra exposes our inability to pinpoint with exactitude the official outset of such phenomenon. Ironically, the first documented "immigration problem" between Mexico and Texas seems to have concerned the Mexican government in the 1820s. In a flagrant case of illegal immigration, large numbers of Anglo-Americans were then crossing the northern and eastern Texas borders looking to establish unapproved settlements in these then-Mexican northernmost territories.[23]

After the American Civil War, Mexicans were "vigorously recruited [...] to the newer cotton region of central Texas, to help family farmers chop (weed) and pick their cotton."[24] This marked the dawn of a long history of alternating attraction and repulsion of Mexican farm and industrial labor to and from the United States on an as-needed basis, as dictated by economic cycles producing either abundance or shortages in the supply of labor force. In fact,

---

22. Coerver, Don M., and Linda B. Hall. Texas and the Mexican Revolution: A Study in State and National Border Policy, 1910-1920. San Antonio, TX: Trinity UP, 1984, 8.

23. Henderson, Timothy J. A Glorious Defeat: Mexico and its war with the United States. New York: Hill and Wand, 2008, 49-50.

24. Foley, Neil. The White Scourge: Mexicans, Blacks, And Poor Whites in Texas Cotton Culture. Berkeley: University of California Press, 1997. eBook Collection (EBSCOhost), 25 (accessed November 1, 2016).

the Immigration Act of 1864, or "An act to encourage immigration"[25] reveals the importance lawmakers placed on immigrants not only as a solution for labor shortages caused by the Civil War, but also as guarantors of economic development in postbellum times.

The year of 1882 was pivotal in reshaping the until then rudimentary immigration policy of the United States. While northern Europeans were arriving in the country via its Atlantic ports of entry, a large number of Chinese nationals began entering it, mainly through San Francisco. The opportunities arising in the newly acquired California territories, allied to conjunctural socio-economic conditions in a few of the most populated Chinese provinces, contributed with the push and pull factors to this increased wave of immigration across the Pacific Ocean.

The ever-greater integration of Chinese citizens in the workforce soon triggered a sentiment of hostility on the part of the Anglo-American population who opposed the presence of the Chinese on American soil on the basis of, among other factors, racial inferiority— which culminated in the Chinese Exclusion Act of 1882. The first relevant consideration to draw from such legislation is the fact that it set a precedent of socially and ethnically-motivated stance towards immigration in the United States. The period of so-called "unrestricted immigration" between 1850 and 1882 had ended. On the other hand, this also signified the inception of a system of border administration, and therefore marked the establishment of border

---

25. President Lincoln, in addressing Congress in 1863, advocated for "the expediency of establishing a system for the encouragement of immigration," which he found necessary due to "the great deficiency of laborers in every field of industry, especially in agriculture and our mines, as well of iron and coal as of the precious metals" (Abraham Lincoln: "Third Annual Message," December 8, 1863. Online by Gerhard Peters and John T. Woolley, The American Presidency Project. presidency.ucsb.edu/ws/?pid=29504. Accessed October 5, 2017).

controls.[26] As a first and immediate consequence, "excludable" immigrants barred from entering the country via its western seaports were redirected to its ground borders with Canada and Mexico.[27]

It is not without irony that the Mexican border witnessed the most clandestine crossings among Chinese nationals— and later by Europeans and Syrians— before Mexicans themselves began their surreptitious journey north in more massive numbers. Waves of immigrants from Europe, Asia, and Africa arrived in Mexican seaports on both its Atlantic and the Pacific coasts to then enter the United States by crossing the U.S.-Mexican land border in California and Texas. The Mexican corridors gained further demand as stronger enforcement controls along the Canadian border were adopted, as well as the increased "head-tax" (in 1903) applied to non-Mexican or non-Canadian foreigners entering the United States via the respective borders. The argument could then be made that the heightening of the restrictions on Asian immigration at the U.S.-Mexican border also created a void which Mexican peasants began filling in more significant numbers by the turn of the century. The increased pattern of Mexican immigration had its roots on both sides of the border.

Admittedly, the presidency of Porfirio Díaz[28] and its liberal economic policies provided push factors in the sense that with land ownership concentrated in the hands of a few — *latifundios* —, former peasant landowners were displaced in large numbers and encouraged to head to Mexico's northern states to work in railroad

26. Ettinger, Patrick W. Imaginary Lines: Border Enforcement and the Origins of Undocumented Immigration, 1882-1930. Austin: U of Texas, 2009, 20.

27. Ettinger 38.

28. José de la Cruz Porfirio Díaz Mori served a total of seven terms as the President of Mexico, or 35 years, between 1876 and 1911. Even though the Porfiriato, as the period of his rule is often called, saw significant economic progress and modernization, these gains did not correlate with social progress, as the benefits of the economic boom were felt by few of his fellow citizens.

construction— a flagship project of Díaz's plan to modernize the country. With this displacement also came inflation and a decline in wages, and workers quickly learned of even better opportunities in rail work, mining, and agriculture across the border in the American Southwest. The chief pull factors were, besides the void created by the backlash against Asians, the expansion of the railroad system. On one hand, these ventures constituted a magnet for labor; on the other, they later provided traveling convenience that facilitated migration (including in Mexico, where railroad track was laid with mostly American investment capital).[29] In addition, large-scale appropriation of land in California destined to intensive agriculture also played its role in pulling migrants across the southern border.

Quantifying the extent to which Mexicans crossed the border into the United States, for seasonal work or otherwise, during the first decade of the 20th century is virtually impossible, as the United States Bureau of Immigration did not keep records of Mexican immigrants crossing the border until 1908. In turn, non-immigrant crossings (i.e., mainly migrant labor) were not tallied until 1911.[30] In any case, it is important to point out that the vast majority of this border-crossing venture was circular, meaning that most migrants viewed their stay in the United States as temporary and therefore planned to return, or eventually did so, to Mexico in the short/medium term. This is also telling of the perception on the part of American authorities that the flux of Mexican citizens into the country did not present a significant problem— at least not until the Mexican Revolution in 1910.

The lack of official bookkeeping in regard to the number of Mexican immigrants and labor workers making their way across the border by no means endorses the sense of preservation of the

29. Henderson, Beyond Borders, 15.
30. Ettinger 126.

unregulated border-crossing tradition of the previous century. During the first decade of the 19th century, the Bureau of Immigration did scrutinize the flow of Mexican citizens seeking to cross the border, which resulted in the debarment of great numbers of prospective immigrants at the most important ports of entry. In this period, debarment and admittance into the country were closely intertwined with labor demands north of the border, as immigration officials were sensitive to the interests of local employers, often at the insistence of the latter, and thus engaged in the *de facto* regulation of the supply of labor. The supply and demand binary thus contributed significantly to "compromising the application of immigration laws to Mexican laborers."[31] In the meantime, exclusion at the port of entry predictably resulted in surreptitious crossings elsewhere, as migrants and immigrants alike would neither have the financial means to afford a return train ticket back to their hometowns in central Mexico nor a way of subsistence on the south side of the borderlands. At the time, there were not any physical barriers in place outside the main border control posts of El Paso, Nogales, Eagle Pass, Laredo, and Brownsville to inhibit illegal crossings. For this reason, it is likely that many Mexican sojourners— precisely how many is anyone's guess— secretly made their way across around those checkpoints. It was not until 1909 when the first "illegal aliens" were apprehended for having evaded inspection and crossed the border illegally, following a more rigid approach in the observance of labor-supply-related scrutiny and control by immigration entities.[32]

The rapid process of industrialization of the late 19th and early 20th centuries in the United States and its consequent demand for labor— and preferably of the cheap kind— continued to provide significant pull factors that incentivized the northbound journey

---

31. Ettinger 134.
32. Ettinger 133.

of significant numbers of laborers from Mexico. In the same vein, the Reclamation Act of 1902 catalyzed the "construction of large-scale irrigation and reclamation projects" in the Southwest, where the availability of an ample and inexpensive labor supply would be needed for the development of the vastly expanded crop area.[33] It is worth noting that the recruitment of labor by American labor agencies in Mexico, sometimes forcefully, was not uncommon, in spite of operating in clear infringement of the law.[34] The perceived need, on the part of Anglo-Americans and more recent European immigrants, for the "protection of American labor via some kind of immigration regulation" continued to contrast with the inconsistency of the rigor applied to the observation of immigration restrictions at the border for a good part of the first quarter-century.[35] Relatedly, Mark Reisler stresses that "employment agencies not only discovered jobs for Mexicans in the United States but also sought out prospective in Mexico and stimulated their emigration. Agents traveled to the *interior* of Mexico (emphasis mine) to spread the news of high American wages," and apparently even "hired workers and arranged their rail passage to the border."[36]

Mexican Revolution (1910-1920s)

---

33. McWilliams, Carey. North from Mexico: The Spanish-speaking People of the United States. New York: Greenwood, 1968, 175.

34. The Foran Act of 1885, most commonly known as Alien Contract Labor Law or Anti-Contract Labor Law, expressly prohibited the importation of labor into the United States— in the form of any kind of assistance, such as transportation or/and offering of contracts, on the part of any American entity to any foreign national not already in the country.

35. Calavita, Kitty. U.S. Immigration Law and the Control of Labor: 1820-1924. London: Academic Press, 1984, 51.

36. Reisler, Mark. By the Sweat of Their Brow: Mexican Immigrant Labor in the United States, 1900-1940. Westport, CT: Greenwood, 1976, 9.

The succession of Profirio Díaz in the presidency of Mexico sparked a civil conflict that had deep roots in the discontent of the destitute masses who never benefited from over three decades of *Porfiriato*. The effects of the Mexican revolution in "an already fragile economy" were devastating: "agricultural production plummeted as unemployment, malnutrition, and prices increased," making "American wages more attractive than ever" to a great number of Mexicans who had remained poor and uneducated during the Díaz's regime and who saw their economic situation deteriorating even further as a result of the political instability.[37] The push northward would not just now have economic and political motives, but also a legitimate foundation on concerns for personal safety and survival.

This period of unrest in Mexico contributed to a drastic reduction of Chinese immigration entering its western seaports headed to the United States in the same way European immigration via the Mexican eastern harbors would come to a halt with the outbreak of World War I. Obliquely, the end of Chinese transit at the border meant that Mexicans would become the quasi-exclusive focus of the efforts of Immigration Service agents stationed on the southern border.

Concurrently, the Mexican domestic unrest also meant the deployment of a contingent of American army personnel along the north side of the border. This unprecedented military presence stationed in the vicinity of the main border entry posts was established to: 1) prevent militia-related smuggling in both directions and 2) to uphold the American official neutrality status regarding the state of violence in which the neighboring nation had submerged. Military units assisted the generally understaffed Immigration Service in weeding out anyone who were perceived as potential militia members or otherwise capable and willing of bearing arms north of the border for less than lawful and legitimate purposes. The most

---

37. Reisler 15.

immediate mission carried out by the military forces was one of dissuading illegal crossings by diverting the Mexican expatriates arriving at the border towards the appropriate bureaucratic routes where
the due process of immigration could be duly performed. In turn,
the role of the immigration officer continued to be largely one of
control rather than deterrence, as debarment was mostly intended
to prevent the diseased from crossing and, as seen above, to monitor
the occasional imbalance in the labor supply, as well as to dissuade
any skirmishes from spilling over across the international line. In
any case, the estimated 10% to 17% rate of rejection[38] of Mexican
citizens applying for entry as immigrants was higher than that of immigrants of other nationalities during the same period— the latter
between 2% and 4%.[39] In the 1910's, the rate of rejection of non-immigrant applicants (meaning seasonal and/or temporary workers)
was also much lower than the former figure above, reflecting more
or less accurately the fluctuation of labor demand as determined by
the succession of distinctive economic cycles. Prior to 1917, 2,000
miles of border between the United States and Mexico were left to
the vigilance of about 60 Bureau of Immigration agents, which indicates that law enforcement was less a contender against illegal crossings than the inconvenience and expense the enterprise implied.[40]

Estimates put the number of Mexicans who migrated into the
United States during the first three decades of the 20th century at 1.5
million.[41] Bailey puts that number at 1 million between 1911 and
1929 alone, as a direct result of the Mexican Revolution.[42] As im-
pressive as it may seem (after all, this represented about 10% of the

38. Common causes for debarment during this time were related mostly to
health issues or justified by indigence.
39. Ettinger 141.
40. Henderson, Beyond Borders, 29.
41. Ettinger 140.
42. Bailey 32.

total Mexican population at the time), the significance of this figure is relative for a few reasons. First, the statistics do not differentiate between immigrants and migrants, which is significant since much of the cross-border traffic during this period was circular, (i.e., many migrants returned to Mexico on a seasonal basis); and second, little data can be found to attest the extent to which destitute peasants returned home to benefit from the "sweeping agrarian reform" and other social programs brought about by the revolution that facilitated the repossession of their livelihoods once the period of violence subsided.[43] In any case, what's important is that most of those who crossed the southern border northward did so *legally*, even when the Immigration Act of 1917 sought to impose severe restrictions on the admittance of Mexican nationals into the United States. Concomitantly, data suggests that among the one million refugees who may have migrated clandestinely into the United States between 1911 and 1929 to escape the violence of the conflict did so with the assistance of a coyote, especially after the enactment in 1917 of the legislation mentioned above.[44]

World War I (1914-1918) and the Immigration Act of 1917

During World War I, overall immigration into the United States dropped, a decrease that was mainly due to restrictions imposed by the American government in terms of how many immigrants to admit per year and of what provenance. In that period, and for the first time, the largest number of immigrants into the United States originated from Mexico, due to the dramatic push factors produced by the Mexican revolution, and the pull factors stemming from labor shortages brought about by the deployment of American men to both the battlefields of Europe and towards better-paying (and often

---

43. Guskin 26.
44. Spener 102.

war-related) industrial jobs up north. Interestingly, however, a few non-economic circumstances were combined to inhibit the growth of that number and even to revert it.

The Immigration Act of 1917, reflecting a sentiment of Nationalism shared with most European nations of the time, stipulated a head-tax of $8 to be applied to Mexican nationals. In addition to this amount to be paid upon entry into the country, it also required that "all immigrants over the age of 16 be literate," demonstrating they could write in any one language.[45] In a country such as Mexico with high levels of illiteracy at this time, and amidst civil unrest that deteriorated the living conditions of the general population to sub-human levels,[46] these requirements were certainly founded on unreasonable expectations. Another formidable blow to the perceived torrent of Mexican immigration into the United States in this period was delivered by the rumor, unfounded or not, that the Department of War was drafting immigrants to be deployed to the war fronts in Europe. The supposed hearsay caused large numbers of immigrants to cross the border southward and return home, adhering to the principle that a known evil is a lesser evil.

The replication of the demographic trends following the establishment of the Treaty of Guadalupe Hidalgo was cause for concern, both on the part of the Department of Labor and the Department of War. These legitimate anxieties regarded the scarcity of labor as it threatened predictable repercussions on the success of the war effort by potentially compromising the stability of the food-supply infrastructure supporting it. Likewise, labor shortages forewarned of adverse effects on the transportation network; disruptions on the construction of the railroad grid were then likely, since both sectors

---

45. Ettinger 142.
46. Most of the active population in Mexico were agricultural laborers earning about 20-25 cents/day.

were largely dependent on the employment of Mexican migrants and immigrants.

Large farming employers, as well as rail and mining concerns, were expeditious in expressing to the government their concerns regarding the negative impact that these pressures on the labor force would create on their industries and, consequently, on the economy and war efforts.[47] Nativist and Restrictionist pressures were no match to the political influence exerted by large interest groups who favored unrestricted immigration from Mexico. A mostly free, northbound flow of Mexican workers was indeed fundamental to the pursuit of higher profits, and so labor interests showed no scruples in likening their success with the superior interests of the nation. As a result, just three months after the legislation had been passed, the Department of Labor gave in to the demands of landowners and railroad tycoons for Mexican nationals to be exempted from the "head tax, literacy test, and contract labor clauses" stipulated in the Immigration Act.[48] Waivers to these provisions still attempted to preserve six-month contract limitations, but the continuous pressure from the part of the private sector cleared these immigration hurdles as well, guaranteeing that the exemptions be granted until 1922, well after the end of WWI. By placing labor needs before the letter of law, these waivers effectively embodied a temporary-worker arrangement, arguably the unofficial predecessor of a future bracero program.

Equally indicative of the importance of the Mexican workforce presence in the United States were the public relations initiatives in which civil and military authorities engaged to debunk initial reports that the American military had been conscripting non-citizens.[49]

---

47. Ettinger 142-43.
48. Ettinger 143.
49. Henderson, Beyond Borders, 32.

Along with the waivers to the newer labor laws of the land, these campaigns effectively curbed the departure of a significant portion of the Mexican workforce, thus safeguarding the ongoing expansion of the American economy and, arguably, assuring the adequate supply of military personnel necessary to the success of its war effort abroad. In any case, it is unquestionable that the vigor of the restrictions to unauthorized immigration and the level of repression adopted to curb it fluctuated according to the labor needs of farmers and industry in the United States on the heels of the alternating economic cycles.

Post WWI into the 1920s

With the end of the war in Europe in 1917 and the normalization of transoceanic traffic came the resumption of the flow of European and Asian immigrants trying to reach the United States via Mexican seaports and, subsequently, its northern border. This period also coincided with a relative reduction in unrest associated with the Mexican Revolution, making such enterprise somewhat safer than in previous years. This created both the conditions for an increased pressure on the Immigration Services at the U.S. southern border and the resurgence of natural incentives for illegal crossings. This was especially true considering the discriminatory immigration requirements aimed at the exclusion of certain groups. However, the economic boom spurred by the end of the war was short-lived, and the wave of unemployment that stemmed from the depression of 1920-21 exposed many Mexican immigrants to a heightened sentiment of rejection, discrimination, and repulsion. This stance led to the repatriation of thousands back to Mexico, a process less onerous and costly than would be that of deporting European and Asian immigrants. Meanwhile, as Ettinger observes citing the Annual Report of the Commissioner-General of Immigration of 1920, an estimated

60,000 immigrants (mostly Mexican) crossed the border illegally between July of 1919 and June of 1920 through the entry port of Laredo alone— arguably encouraged by continued unrealistic immigration policies, as well as inconsistent dispositions aimed at its deterrence.[50]

In 1921, as a reaction to the labor surplus and in the wake of a rise in power and influence of advocates of immigration restrictions, Congress enacted immigration legislation known as the "Emergency Quota Law." The new law set the limit on the number of "aliens" to be admitted into the United States at 3% of the total foreign-born resident population of the same nationality— based on the census of 1910. Interestingly, however, the provisions of the law granted exemptions to, among others, Cubans, Mexicans, and Central and South Americans. The exemption was arguably a sign of a not-so-masked legislative attempt to specifically exclude immigrants from Southern and Eastern Europe, on the heels of a feared potential increase of postwar immigration originating in said regions.[51] The quantitative restrictions reinforced the natural invitation for illegal crossing and smuggling, not only of Mexicans, but especially of many Europeans and Asians who saw their prospects of legal admittance considerably reduced by the newly enacted legislation. Once again, it is clear that unauthorized entry in the early years of the 20th century was hardly exclusive to Mexican nationals. On one hand, Europeans and Asians did so to circumvent immigration policies designed to debar their entry; on the other, Mexicans were being discouraged from following the proper legal channels mainly because the absence of effective physical barriers at the border made it more convenient and expeditious to cross unregulated.[52] Furthermore, it is important

---

50. Ettinger 151.

51. Calavita 149.

52. An argument could be made here for the technical distinction between illegal and unregulated border crossing.

to acknowledge that after World War I, and notably in periods of economic growth, the incentives for the preference of unsupervised border crossing were not the same for all groups.

While the new immigration control measures were initially met with ambivalence by industrial tycoons, mainly due to the lower demand for labor dictated by the economic downturn, it did not take long before the private sector disavowed these restrictions for being the root cause of worrisome labor shortages. By the time the economic cycle turned around and the economy began rebounding around 1923, industry moguls became particularly concerned with the upward pressures a labor shortfall would inflict on wages, rather than with an actual paralysis of economic activity due to workforce scarcity.[53] The need for an abundant labor supply associated with foreign-born manpower would thus not be in dispute during the roaring twenties; rather, at the center of the debate was the devising of effective mechanisms to attract and keep the right kind of "immigrants"— debate which would inevitably continue to be reflected in legislative initiatives and immigration policies for years to come. The right kind of immigrants were, it could be argued, those "without the political and economic strains associated with immigrants from the more permanent European source" but at the same time,

---

53. While agriculture provided the main drive for the presence of Mexican migrants and immigrants in the United States, by no means were they absent from other domains of economic activity in the country. According to Herbert Gutman, for instance, "35% of Chicago Inland Steel's work force was Mexican" in 1926. The shift from rural to urban areas of the country on the part of large number of Mexican immigrants in the early twenties is also attributed to the economic depression of 1920-21, which had particularly devastating effects on agricultural production of the southwest, thus causing massive unemployment in a sector largely dependent on immigrant and/or migrant labor (Gutman, Herbert G. Work, Culture, and Society in Industrializing America: Essays in American Working-class and Social History. New York: Knopf, 1976, 8).

paradoxically, also least likely to assimilate: migrant workers from across the southern border.[54]

In this context, and as the "recruitment of Mexican workers resumed with vigor" in 1923, the political pressure for the creation of a border patrol increased.[55] The establishment of a force to guard against illicit entry on both the Mexican and Canadian borders reveals the diverse origin of the surreptitious crossers. In fact, Mexican nationals entering the United States were not seen as a major immigration problem by the competent authorities at the local level. This was because top economic players— both agriculturalists in the Southwest and industry employers elsewhere— had made a convincing case of the advantages of a permeable border to migrant workers from the south. The (perceived) status of temporary labor provided by workers of Mexican origin continued to be the source of positive discrimination bestowed upon these nationals, although this expediency was limited to the time of entry and did not reflect later on higher wages or better living conditions and social acceptance. In fact, the dissemination of the notion, objectionable in every way, of Mexicans as racially inferior beings helped maintain a regime of exception for those nationals substantiated in a relatively unrestricted admittance praxis at the border. Moreover, this condescending social stance was also bound to justify the wretched living quarters, low wages, and arduous working conditions to which Mexican immigrants were subjected. At the same time, it fostered a state of dependency for so-called unskilled labor from the neighboring south.

In a memorable instance, the vigorous protests by cotton growers of Imperial Valley, California, became legendary in the aftermath of the raids performed on their fields in the fall of 1925 by immigration authorities in search of undocumented workers. The backlash

---

54. Calavita 157.
55. Reisler 55.

created by the initiative, which resulted in the detention of a large number of undocumented workers, reverberated all the way to the Labor Department.[56] Indeed, cotton growers compelled labor authorities to require the Immigration Service be more judicious in their enforcement of the law by taking heed of the prevailing interests of the employers. As a compromise, California growers acted as intermediaries between their workers and the Immigration Service and facilitate the proper legalization of the former by collecting, on behalf of the latter, the amounts equivalent to what these workers failed to render at the border upon bypassing the legal entry channels and proceedings.[57] This arrangement seemed to appease some, but infuriated Texan growers who saw the deal as allowing an unfair advantage to their competitors in California.

By this time, the American agrarian sector was so dependent on the seasonal labor provided by Mexican migrant workers that farmers farther north began competing with growers from the Southwest for the procurement of Mexican workers during harvest time. The situation became so dire that the state of Texas actually enacted legislation— the Emigrant Agent Act of 1929— to curb the loss of migrant labor to growers from contiguous states and beyond by inhibiting the recruiting of workers in the region.[58]

As the National Origins Act of 1924 sought to extend and strengthen similar legislation from 1921 by further stifling the flow of Southern European and Asian immigration into the United States, the encouragement for surreptitious crossings through the U.S.–Mexican border on the part of these nationals was reinforced. Furthermore, fears of insecurity associated with the Mexican revolution were residual since skirmishes were by this time sporadic

---

56. Reisler 61.

57. Reisler 62-63.

58. Reisler 58.

and generally inconsequential. Although exempt from the new 2% foreign-born quota limitations,[59] the stipulations for the legal admittance of Mexican nationals into the United States were burdened by bureaucracy, expense, and long waiting times. This situation continued to add poorer Mexicans to the roll of prospective illegal border crossers along with Japanese, Chinese, Spaniards, Italians, Portuguese, and Greeks. The heightened demand for clandestine crossings also conferred further vitality and profit to resourceful ventures offering to meet the needs of those seeking illegal and surreptitious entry since the beginning of the establishment of restrictive border policies, i.e., the coyotes. Lucrative human smuggling enterprises facilitated the clandestine entry of thousands of Europeans and Asians along both the Canadian and the Mexican borders for much of the 1920s.[60] Meanwhile, it is fair to suppose that undocumented crossing of Mexicans also gained a new breadth with the establishment of visa requirements in 1925,[61] possibly in direct proportion to the steep reduction on the number of legally admitted Mexican migrants and immigrants.

The creation of a border patrol finally came to fruition in 1924, in the context of the debate surrounding the National Origins Act.[62] Pressured by a few restrictionist politicians, Congress approved the

---

59. By 1924, Mexicans were considered "white", but labor pressures arguably contributed just as much as this ethnical classification to their exemption, as well as to nationals from the rest of the hemisphere, from the quota limits imposed by the National Origins Act of that year.

60. Ettinger 152.

61. Ettinger 151. Legal Mexican immigrants were required, starting in 1925, to obtain a visa at one of the American consulates in Mexico, incurring in an additional $10 expense on top of the $8 head-tax to be disbursed upon entry at the border.

62. "Border Patrol History." U.S. Customs and Border Protection. U.S. Department of Homeland Security, (n/d), cbp.gov/border-security/along-us-borders/history (accessed October 24, 2017).

strengthening of border enforcement with additional funding and manpower, which laid the provisions for an *ad hoc* border policing force. Since the passage of the Eighteenth Amendment in 1919, a surge in bi-directional border-crossing traffic raised fears of increased northbound human and alcohol smuggling dissimulated as legitimate transit.[63] However, testimonial accounts acknowledged that the border patrol "put significantly less effort into detaining undocumented Mexican workers than to catching European and Asian aliens" in the first years after its inception.[64] Any increase in the number of patrolling agents would render insufficient to cover the immense length of territory that constitutes the border between the U.S. and its neighbors both to the south and to the north. As such, very early on the border patrol adopted a strategy that embraced the unforgiving terrain of the Southwest as natural allies in its efforts to inhibit illegal crossings. Patrolling thus tended to focus on areas around the main ports of entry, while mountainous and desert areas remained largely unsupervised. In the meantime, coeval reports persisted in pointing to large numbers of illegal immigrants not only from Mexico, but also from Europe and Asia, permeating both borders, either by circumventing inspection or by deceiving the inspectors several years after the establishment of a dedicated border patrol. The founding of this agency never thwarted the political endeavors of the largest American employers and their associations to undermine stricter immigration controls and enforcement, insofar as the status quo served their economic interests.

---

63. The amendment was ratified on January 16, 1919, and took effect one year later. The Volstead Act of October of 1919 defined the more specific terms of what became known as Prohibition, which banned the manufacture or sale of "intoxicating liquors" in the United States other than those used for medicinal purposes.
64. Ettinger 162.

Thus, much of the undocumented migration and immigration of Mexicans into the United States also in this period "arose from the intersection of labor market demand, the desire for family re-unification, and erection of 'artificial barriers' of immigration laws."[65] Furthermore, the inability of the Immigration Service to respond adequately to the high volume of aspiring immigrants arriving at the border on a daily basis added to the problem and further encouraged illicit entry. The inconsistency of admittance control mechanisms displayed at the border helped "foster migration traditions and net-works" which fortified the foundation for "considerable smuggling of aliens and undocumented entry in the1920s" and persisted to a certain degree after the creation of the border patrol.[66]

During the second half of the decade, growers in the Southwest continued to face off with immigration restrictionists in Washington, who by mid-decade had begun to endorse enthusiastically the idea of imposing tighter restrictions on the lawful admission of Mexican immigrants in the United States. By virtue of the aforementioned growers' pressure against further immigration constraints, Congress failed to approve any legislation aimed at revoking the exemptions enacted by the Emergency Quota Law of 1921 and later retained by the National Origins Act of 1924.[67] Instead of policy, tighter re-strictions came by way of procedure, and so the issuance of visas at the consulates in Mexico found itself under more scrutiny by 1928.[68] A more rigorous disposition in the application of the legal require-ments for prospective immigrants was thus followed, not surprising-ly, by a dramatic decline in the number of immigrant visas issued by decade's end. Simultaneously, border patrol duties were carried out

---

65. Ettinger 152.
66. Ettinger 152.
67. Reisler 58-59.
68. Reisler 214.

with unprecedented zeal after 1929 in sharp contrast with the permissiveness displayed in previous years. The Registry Act of March, 1929, further represents a vehement opposition to the presence of undesired aliens in the country. The new legislation criminalized the entry without inspection of non-citizens as a misdemeanor and established a penalty of imprisonment of up to two years to those aliens attempting reentry after being deported.[69] While allowing some immigrants to obtain legal status, few Mexicans benefited from the opportunity offered by the Registry Act, as "the largest number of applications came from European immigrants, who accounted for some 80 percent of those whose status was regularized."[70]

The Great Depression (1929-1939)

The Great Depression and the economic woes it created would prove far more effective in curbing the flow of Mexican labor into the United States than any enforcement measures at the border or elsewhere. Because of massive unemployment among American citizens throughout all sectors of the economy, many began competing for jobs that were previously only attractive to immigrants. This sudden imbalance of supply and demand of labor meant a significant downward pressure on wages, in addition to significantly reduced northbound migration flows. Not only did the new arrival of Mexican workers come to a halt during the years of the depression, an estimated 400,000 Mexican citizens were repatriated — voluntarily or forcefully— in the first few years of the 1930s, reflecting the anti-immigrant sentiment that prevailed during these times of economic collapse.[71] This ethos was often expressed in anti-immigrant raids and other terrorist activities led by civilians aimed at intimidating

---

69. Reisler 214.
70. Henderson, Beyond Borders, 43.
71. Ettinger 168.

and eventually leading to voluntary repatriation of immigrants. At the official level, California, Arizona, and Illinois enacted legislation in the beginning of that decade "requiring that all laborers on public works projects be U.S. citizens," further barring Mexicans from the unskilled labor market that had previously sought to employ them.[72] In the meantime, the federal government was doing its part in discouraging immigration from the south, namely by refusing visas for legitimate entry and employment, but also by intensifying the deportation efforts of "undesirable aliens," either by effective removal or by use of scare tactics. At the same time, Mexican migrants and immigrants were feeling the leverage at employability they previously enjoyed (easy deportation, as opposed to European and Asian immigrants) turning against them. Furthermore, local authorities strived to reduce the welfare burden that thousands of unemployed or inadequately-paid Mexicans represented to public coffers by pressuring those nationals into leaving the United States.

Fallen from grace, a large number of Mexicans were repatriated during these distressing times of economic uncertainty; extreme poverty and social isolation forced many to migrate to northern inner cities to join the large ranks of those who found themselves dispossessed and disfranchised.

World War II (1939-1945) and the Bracero Program (1942-1964)

The beginning of World War II brought about an economic boom that would lift the American economy out of the Great Depression. While the defense industry provided abundant job opportunities to many whom the economic collapse had left unemployed, Mexican workers did not benefit significantly from the potential higher wages that a short labor supply would usually entail. As early as 1942, growers in the Southwest lobbied the Roosevelt administration to adopt a system to expedite the admittance of migrant workers into

---

72. Reisler 228.

the country to preserve the bountiful supply of unskilled labor that kept wages low: the *Bracero* Program was born.[73] Mexican workers were once again in high demand, not only in agriculture, but also in railroad work, the military service, and in industries closely associated with the war effort. Portrayed as a temporary wartime measure, the program sought to admit seasonal agricultural workers, similar to the approach during World War I, when exemptions allowed to significantly ease the hurdles to the admittance of Mexican workers into the American unskilled job market. The effect of the program on the number of *braceros* crossing the border proved to be of a greater scale than that seen during the first wartime experiment. Different versions of the program were successively adopted before its termination by the end of 1964, 4 million signed contracts later and almost 20 years after the end of the war.[74]

If the reported goal of the *Bracero* Program was to curtail illegal immigration, then its effects fell short, contributing instead to a sharp increase in undocumented border crossings. The mere existence of the *Bracero* Program effectively signaled the abundance of job opportunities across the border to poorer Mexicans, many of whom made the trip north with disregard to the official contractual proceedings dictated by the program. Moreover, as employers viewed the provisions of the program as "socialistic" demands (i.e. burdens interfering with their pursuit of maximum efficiency and

---

73. In the meantime, economic conditions in Mexico were still poor mainly because the promising reforms carried out during the presidency of Lázaro Cárdenas (1934-1940) mostly favored foreign corporations and other large economic interests. As the wealth failed to trickle down to the general population following sweeping agrarian reforms, famine was a regular occurrence even in years of record agricultural output. In these conditions, many poverty-stricken Mexicans were highly motivated to take extreme measures to improve their livelihood and venture north.

74. Ettinger 168.

profit), they welcomed undocumented workers with open arms. The apparent impunity of this stratagem was reinforced by the nature of the sanctions imposed on those caught working illegally: enrollment in the program *post factum*.[75] In the same vein, border patrol officers were discretionary in their approach to illegal crossing in this period, acting permissively in cases where it was apparent that undocumented border-crossers were farm workers and tending to apprehend those whom they deemed as mere vagabonds. The leniency displayed by the border patrol post-World War II is analogous to that encouraged by Southwestern landowners during the first global conflict and the period of economic growth (i.e. higher labor demand) preceding the financial collapse of 1929. In fact, the number of parallel undocumented workers in the United States during the first ten years of the *Bracero* Program is estimated to have surpassed that of official contractual labor, judging by the substantial rise in the recorded number of apprehensions at the border for illegal crossing attempts during that period.[76] Likewise, the number of legalized undocumented migrant workers surpassed that of new recruits after 1949.[77]

In 1951, the United States and Mexico renegotiated the terms of the Bracero Program. Under pressure from American Restrictionists in Washington, the agreement included language to make it illegal to "import" or "harbor" illegal migrants. But growers from Texas made sure to protect their interests and lobbied against the association between "hiring" and "importing" or "harboring" under the

---

75. Ettinger 169.

76. Texas growers not only attempted to weaken the terms of the program in their favor, they refused to participate in it until the 1950s— while showing a clear preference for recruiting and hiring undocumented workers instead, thus avoiding bureaucratic hurdles and more easily dodging labor regulations stipulated by the terms of the agreement.

77. Ettinger 169.

law.[78] Likewise, proposed amendments to criminalize the hiring of undocumented individuals were eventually defeated, thus preserving employers' ability to continue hiring unauthorized workers with impunity.

Two years later, Mexican authorities, aware that the hiring of Mexican workers outside of the realm of the bi-national agreement was conducive to abuses of all kinds, set out to persuade their American counterparts to penalize employers who engaged in such practice. As the negotiating leverage enjoyed by Mexico in the first few years of the program waned, the United States wavered regarding Mexico's demands for higher wages and decent living conditions for its workers under the program. When Mexico refused to extend the agreement past 1954, the United States decided to reserve for itself the right to decide on the fate of the labor agreement without Mexican interference. Accordingly, the Departments of Justice, Labor, and State jointly declared that the country would continue to hire *braceros* unilaterally, regardless of Mexico's official stance. This incident eventually took an ironic twist when Mexican troops were deployed to the border to forcefully bar Mexican citizens from crossing it, while border patrol agents on the United States side extended their open arms to any Mexican who attempted to enter the country to join the ranks of *braceros*.

Away from the border, however, animosity towards immigrants grew steadily during the 1950s, both as a result of an economic deceleration and the nationalistic fervor associated with the Cold

---

78. Henderson, Beyond Borders, 78. During the renegotiation of the Bracero Program in the 1950s, Congress conceded to Mexico's demands and approved a bill making it a felony to harbor and conceal illegal entrants. A delegation representing Texan growers in the negotiation process demanded the inclusion of language stating that employing illegal immigrants did not constitute "harboring and concealing" them, a stipulation markedly directed at freeing its proponents from liability that became known as the Texas Proviso.

War mindset of the period. In this context, and because they always made good scapegoats of the economic and financial woes of the country, Congress once again passed legislation targeting illegal migrants— but without inflicting further legal inconveniences on the farm lobby. For example, one of the mandates established that employers were not to hire undocumented workers, but cynically relieved them from the burden of thoroughly verifying the legal status of anyone who produced documentation for employment.[79] These mandates not only effectively empowered growers to continue hiring virtually any migrants they desired, they also opened the door to the possibility of wage theft. Routinely, less-than-scrupulous employers questioned the authenticity of the worker's documentation *after* the harvest, only to use their illegal status as pretext to deny them the wages they were due.

Provisions in the new legislation nevertheless strengthened controls at the border. The renewed resolve triggered Operation Wetback, a law enforcement initiative implemented in 1954 that vastly expanded the raids, arrests, mass roundup, and deportation of undocumented workers mostly from the California and Texas border areas, but also from the metropolitan areas of Los Angeles, San Francisco, and Chicago. The Immigration and Naturalization Service (INS) claimed to have deported or driven to voluntary return to Mexico about 1.3 million undocumented workers during the Operation Wetback.[80] By virtue of the prestige it gained in the wake of the reported success of the operation, the Border Patrol also saw its funding increase, a contributing factor to the lasting effect of a more permanent and substantial border control presence along the international divide after the 1950s. In the meantime, though, regulations inherent to the *Bracero* Program were weakened to appease

---

79. Henderson, Beyond Borders, 84.
80. Henderson, Beyond Borders, 85.

Southwest farmers, many of whom saw leniency in the law as an opportunity to engage in or continue abusive labor practices.

The 22 years in which the *Bracero* Program was law further contributed to a status quo of mutual labor dependency between migrant workers from the south and employers from the north, one that would have lasting effects for years to come. As Mexican families became dependent on seasonal work north of the border, American farmers had grown reliant on the cheap labor provided by the *braceros* in times of most need. In this sense, the *Bracero* Program proved to be a camouflaged "massive government subsidy to powerful [American] farming interests."[81] In fact, the farm lobby greatly appreciated both the downward pressure on wages bolstered by abundant labor and the light obligations they faced regarding workers' rights. This was especially true regarding a workforce comprised of undocumented migrants working and living in deplorable conditions. The prevalence of this supply-and-demand system of labor would persist in the decades following the termination of the very program that helped its consolidation, thus perpetuating seasonal migration patterns well beyond 1964. Foreign workers from south of the border saw the number of opportunities to work legally in the United States fall precipitously after Congress unilaterally terminated the program. The rise in the number of apprehensions along the border was thus consistent with the predictable growth of illegal migration in the wake of the cessation of this bi-national labor agreement.

Immigration and Nationality Act of 1965

After the end of the *Bracero* Program in 1964, the Immigration and Nationality Act of 1965 is the next landmark in the history of illegal immigration from the south. A more liberal mindset among

---

81. Henderson, Beyond Borders, 88.

legislators in Washington favored the end of the "national origins" quota of 1924 and called for a more inclusive immigration policy. With that in mind, the new law set equal quotas for immigrants regardless of their country of origin, albeit ignoring the different levels of demand that closer geographic and economic proximity to the United States would naturally entail. Such was the case of Mexico, which had been traditionally and by far the largest Latin American exporter of immigrants to the United States. Levelling numbers for allowed immigration from Mexico, in clear dissonance with relatively higher demand, meant that most immigration from the southern neighbor was now effectively *illegal*.

In the meantime, and in spite of increasing Gross Domestic Product growth, sustained mainly by a rather vigorous process of industrialization, Mexico's economy was failing to reflect these gains onto the working classes. In fact, by mid-20th century, Mexico maintained the most unequal distribution of wealth in the world, contrasting the highest GDP in Latin America with the smallest budgets for education and other social services in the region.[82] By this time, the number of applicants for legal immigration from Mexico had also surpassed that of any other country.[83]

Put together, these two factors caused the number of apprehensions and deportations at the border to skyrocket after 1968,[84] mainly between Tijuana and San Diego. This was naturally revealing of an ever-larger number of Mexicans motivated to seek better wages north of the border. The economic crisis impacting Mexico during the 1970s and 1980s, mostly as the natural outcome of the failed

---

82. Henderson, Beyond Borders, 92.

83. Yang, Philip Q. Post-1965 Immigration to the United States: Structural Determinants. Westport, CT: Praeger, 1995, 15.

84. During the more critical years of the Cold War, the fear of enemy infiltration through the southern border called for a heightened level of border surveillance, as well as to an increased scrutiny of crossers.

social and labor policies of the preceding decades, added to the pressure so that the number of illegal immigrants from Mexico continued to rise throughout the period.

As American agriculture became increasingly mechanized, the need for intensive labor was decreased in some cultures, and so the new wave of immigrants began seeking employment in larger numbers in other sectors of the economy, mostly services and light industry, and farther from the points of entry into the country. This expanded geographic distribution added visibility to the presence of illegal immigrants in the United States, eventually leading to the association of the phenomenon with Mexicans in the collective perception of American society. These greater social concerns, sometimes exaggerated, echoed in the chambers of governance, where some legislators repeatedly advanced proposals to criminalize the hiring of illegal immigrants as a way to uproot the greatest incentive to their presence. Like twenty years prior, congressmen with strong ties to agribusiness and other interest groups that saw employer sanctions as a threat vehemently opposed these legislative initiatives and successfully pushed for their demise. Failing to provide a path to legalization while at the same time signaling for the economic viability of their work, American society continued to force these immigrants to live and work in the shadows of society, while arguably contributing more to the sustainability of its lifestyle than taking from the common pool of its social contract. The influx of refugees from Indochina, Cuba, and Haiti into the United States during the first years of the 1980s reinforced the anti-immigrant sentiment and fueled restrictionist voices in opposition to immigration in general. These hostile outcries were eventually met with Supreme Court rulings affirming the protection of the basic human rights of immigrants.

Immigration Reform and Control Act of 1986

Towards the end of 1986, Ronald Reagan signed into law the Immigration Reform and Control Act, also known as Simpson-Mazzoli Act in honor of its two sponsors, with the dual purpose of controlling and deterring illegal immigration to the United States.

The IRCA granted legal status to all illegal immigrants who proved to be in the country continuously since before January 1, 1982 and who were guiltless of crimes. To benefit from the amnesty, undocumented immigrants also had to demonstrate a minimal knowledge of U.S. history and government, as well as an acceptable command of English in addition to accepting to pay a fine and taxes due retroactively.

At the same time, the law required employers to validate the immigration status of their employees, making it illegal to hire undocumented workers *knowingly*. The inclusion of the adverb "knowingly" constituted a crucial concession to interest groups with political clout in Washington, since it allowed employers to claim having in good-faith required employees to produce documentation attesting to their legal status without the burden of verifying the authenticity of such documentation, thus rendering the abolition of the Texas Proviso inconsequential. Furthermore, the inclusion in the law of a provision allowing for a more unrestricted legalization of agricultural migrant workers makes even more obvious the influence agricultural syndicates exercised, as they had in the past, in defense of their own interests.

A third major component of the law was directed at enhancing border security, giving in to fears, albeit lacking in foundation and even less material consequence, of enemy infiltration through the southern borders. This anxiety was reminiscent of that lived during the 1920s and again in the 1950s, and one which has never gone out of fashion to this day.[85] To that effect, border control operations saw its funding substantially increased, which may have had an effect, however residual, on the volume of illegal crossings. The expanded level of border surveillance and the restrictions placed on incoming immigrants caused, however, a decrease in seasonal migration, whereby migrants had stronger reasons either to stay in the country longer or make their sojourn permanent. More significantly, they began bringing their families along with them. Another relevant impact of the heightened border vigilance was that it increased the risk and expense associated with unauthorized crossings experienced by undocumented migrants.

In spite of the bureaucratic hurdles and considerable expense imposed by the amnesty, about 3 million immigrants obtained legal status under the IRCA, which also had the unintended consequence of catalyzing an industry dedicated to the forging and marketing of counterfeit documentation.[86]

On a different front, but with similar implications, U.S. historical support for repressive governments in Central America, generally designed to protect American corporate and geopolitical interests in the region, began to bear its bitterest fruit in the 1980s in the form of a sharp rise in immigration originating in Honduras, Nicaragua, Guatemala, and El Salvador— countries which until then had provided a negligible contribution to the bulk of border crossing into the United States.[87] Many of the displaced naturally resorted

---

85. At the time this text is being revised, it is the Islamic terrorists who are feared to have infiltrated the caravan of migrants heading north, mostly from Honduras, and are leading the "invasion" of the country, according to the rhetoric of the Administration.

86. Henderson, Beyond Borders, 115.

87. As global financial institutions (such as the World Bank and the International Monetary Fund) impose economic reforms on poor countries usually aimed at advancing the interests of large corporations in wealthy nations,

to doing so surreptitiously, especially since the Reagan administration refused to grant asylum to these refugees, in contravention with the stipulations of the Refugee Act which President Carter signed in 1980.[88]

Immigration Act of 1990

Enacted in November of 1990, the new Immigration Act sought to complement the IRCA of 1986, although it mostly amended the Immigration and Nationality Act of 1965. After addressing illegal immigration four years before, Congress focused its attention not only on adjusting the legal preferences for admission of immigrants to the United States, but also on the number of immigrants to be allowed per year and the rules governing the naturalization process of non-natural born citizens. At the time of the signing of the bill, President George H. W. Bush stressed the role of the new legislation in welcoming "increased immigration of skilled individuals to meet our economic needs," which highlighted once more the anti-labor mindset underlying U.S. immigration policy.

The Immigration Act once more included provisions aimed at strengthening border patrol and immigration enforcement by budgeting for an increased number of agents on the ground. This added funding, coupled with stricter rules and more expeditious deportation procedures, was followed by an increased number of

---

the populations of the former tend to react against their precarious condition. Bacon emphasizes that in the case of "El Salvador, Guatemala, and Nicaragua, when people tried to upend that social order, they confronted not just the armies of their own elites but, often, U.S. military intervention. Those wars also produced displacement and migration" (Bacon 69).

88. I will return to this issue below and explore in a little more detail some of the socioeconomic and political developments in Central America at the root of such fluxes, culminating more recently in the signing of CAFTA— the Central America Free Trade Agreement.

apprehensions at the border, perhaps in correlation with an elevated number of illicit crossing attempts that may have had its inception before 1990. Operation Blockade[89] and others like it became the most visible side of the strengthened mechanisms of extended border control and criminalization of unauthorized immigration implemented in 1993 in the wake of a surge in anti-immigrant sentiment that characterized this period. Also in 1993, the Border Patrol added hundreds of new agents as its budget continued to swell. This crackdown on the preferred crossing corridors began to force migration fluxes to veer towards the Arizona-Sonora Desert, making the endeavor much more dangerous and the corresponding smuggling fees much higher. This had an unfortunate repercussion on the number of lives claimed by the hazards of the journey— estimated at 10,000 between 1994 and 2018.[90] Phillip Cole highlights the grim contrast between the estimated 400 to 500 deaths per year among illegal migrants attempting to cross the U.S.-Mexico border with the "239 fatalities at the Berlin Wall over 28 years."[91]

Nativists and restrictionists saw worrisome economic indicators developing in the U.S.— rising budget deficits, skyrocketing national debt, and slumping employment numbers— as validation for their arguments. However, contributing decisively to these trends were other factors, such as the deindustrialization of the American econ-

89. Operation Blockade (later renamed Operation Hold-the-line) in Texas (1993), Operation Gatekeeper in California (1994), and Operation Safeguard in Arizona (1994) were a series of aggressive Border Patrol initiatives that resulted from the hostile ethos towards undocumented immigration of the 1990s. A few years later, in 1997, Operation Rio Grande was implemented in South Texas with the similar task of thwarting unsupervised border crossings.
90. Ryon, Sean. "Aid, and agua, along the border." Nation Swell, NationSwell, 11 July 2018, nationswell.com/water-station-mexico-border (accessed December 15, 2018).
91. Wellman, Christopher and Cole, Phillip. Debating the Ethics of Immigration: Is There a Right to Exclude? Oxford University Press, 2011, 283.

omy and its shift to a course of rapid financialization. These processes gained momentum during the Reagan administration and were propelled by an agenda that essentially contributed to the gradual concentration of capital in the hands of few, such as tax cuts for the wealthier Americans, underfunded social programs, and substantial increases in military spending. While this accumulation of capital precipitated the flooding of financial markets, increased industrial competition from abroad inspired much of the American industry to downsize and/or offshore its operations to compensate for loss of profitability. As a result, GDP as a measure of economic growth showed positive signs, although median incomes were falling quickly as most of the gains originated in financial transactions. Predictably, immigrants again provided handy scapegoats for the lost prosperity, even though their raw contribution to the system in the form of direct and indirect taxes paid far surpassed the benefits they reaped in public services. California Proposition 187 (1994) was, in this context, one of the most visible initiatives targeting unauthorized immigrants, as it sought voters' approval to the prohibition of "illegal aliens" from accessing non-emergency healthcare, public education, and an array of other publicly-offered services in the state.[92]

NAFTA

During the earlier years of the 1990s, a wave of economic measures adopted during the presidency of Carlos Salinas were predicated on liberalizing Mexico's economy in an effort to raise the country to the status of industrialized nation. In these circumstances and amidst a period of rare optimistic economic outlook, Mexico began

---

92. The legislative proposal was approved by roughly 59% of California voters, but it was soon found unconstitutional by a federal district court. Nevertheless, the attention received by the referendum helped publicize the issue nationwide and place it in the collective consciousness of the country.

negotiating the terms of the North America Free Trade Agreement (NAFTA) with the United States and Canada. In short, Mexico sought the removal of tariffs to gain further access to U.S. and Canadian markets, while its two commercial partners to the north were focused on opening Mexican doors wider to foreign investment (while guaranteeing its protections), as well as the movement of capital and goods across the border to the south. Needless to say, the free movement of workers was not contemplated in the agreement. Also, "NAFTA provided no social contract," as "it offered neither aid for Mexico nor labor, health or environmental standards."[93] As a result, and not too long after coming into force in January of 1994, economists were able to assess the broader impact of the agreement on the economy of Mexico and its effects on the Mexican population. Although NAFTA contributed to the creation of a meager number of industrial jobs, these were generated mainly by the relocation or outsourcing of American assembly plants[94] lured to Mexico by low wages and lenient regulations, in a grim revival of the darkest side of the Industrial Revolution two hundred years prior. Since these ventures depended, and still do, on low-skilled and generally poorly paid work, they failed on the fundamental NAFTA promise of bringing prosperity to all Mexicans. More importantly, the steep increase in exports failed to trickle down to the general population, rather aggravating income inequality across the board in a country where the

---

93. Faux, Jeff. "How NAFTA Failed Mexico." The American Prospect, TAP, June 16 2003, prospect.org/article/how-nafta-failed-mexico (accessed October 20, 2016).

94. The establishment of maquiladoras, assembly plants that turn imported components into finished products for export, across northern Mexico is a phenomenon that began in the 1960s as part of the Border Industrialization Program spear-headed by the Mexican government. The number of this type of plant along the border expanded substantially in the years following the signing of the free trade agreement: 30% between 1994 and 2000.

distribution of wealth, not only among regions[95] but within society at large, was already sharply uneven. Large agricultural conglomerates were favored by the conditions created with the agreement, forcing many small-scale produce farmers to lay off workers and close farmsteads that had become obsolete in a larger-scale, highly mechanized farming environment. At the same time, the Mexican market was flooded with cheaper corn grown in farms north of the border by more competitive U.S. corporations, bringing a similar fate to many Mexican corn producers. In fact, while the subsidizing of Mexican farmers was ruled illegal, their competitors in the U.S. continued to benefit from the provisions of successive U.S. farm bills, which continued to guarantee huge subsidies to the largest farming interests, further accentuating the asymmetries between growers on each side of the border. This led to the dumping of American agricultural products on the Mexican market in large scale, driving Mexican producers, large and small, out of business. In *Making the Future*, Noam Chomsky points to economist Carlos Salas' assessment that "agricultural employment began to decline when NAFTA came into force" and that the agreement effectively contributed to the displacement of "one-sixth of the Mexican agricultural workforce."[96] Moreover, and as price-control mechanisms were dismantled as part of the neoliberal agenda at the root of NAFTA, the price of consumer goods on staple food items such as tortillas increased steeply, a counterintuitive outcome that intensified poverty and hunger.[97] The

95. Because maquiladoras operated exclusively in areas with easy access to the U.S. market, only the states in northern Mexico benefited from their presence. In the meantime, as economic conditions in states to the south deteriorated, immigrants originating from those regions began arriving in the Unites States in higher numbers than ever before.

96. Chomsky, Noam. Making the Future. San Francisco: City Light Books, 2012, 23.

97. Neoliberalism, as is defined in economic terms, is the ideological heir of

devastating effects of NAFTA were also felt across other sectors of the economy, where depressed wages inevitably incited emigration to the United States.

Before these signs of distress had time to materialize more substantially, a series of circumstances arguably connected with the implementation of NAFTA led to a precipitous depreciation of the Mexican Peso by the end of 1994. The sudden resulting spike in prices devastated an economy heavily dependent on imports of consumer products, resulting in skyrocketing debt and unemployment on a large scale. In addition, and because this type of agreement tends to be supplemented with "structural adjustments" to the economy, the Mexican government embraced policies that effectively eroded protections on workers and producers, further bloating the ranks of the unemployed. Naturally, higher levels of unemployment in Mexico meant a greater incentive to migrate north across the border. In *Illegal People*, David Bacon cogently summarizes this process when he states that "economic reforms promoted by the U.S. government through trade agreements and international financial institutions displace workers, from miners to coffee pickers, who join a huge flood of labor moving north."[98]

Meantime, in the United States, greater immigration pressures directly linked to NAFTA caused anti-illegal immigration endeavors to continue to focus almost exclusively on the border, which, not coincidentally, became increasingly militarized. To that effect, the

---

the "laissez-faire, laissez-passer" economic system introduced in 18th century France. It advocates for a reduced role of government (meaning lax regulations and controls) and for a dominant presence of the private sector in the free-market economy. It is closely associated with the neoconservative movement, which is a proponent of a form of capitalism unhindered by the welfare role of the State, in stark rejection of the Lincolnian vision of a "government of the people, by the people, for the people."

98. Bacon 67.

amount budgeted for border enforcement doubled between 1993 and 1997 (from $400 million to $800 million), reflecting a two-fold increase in the number of border patrol agents on payroll.[99] Higher number of apprehensions resulted in equal measure from the installation of increasingly sophisticated detection devices near and around the main ports of entry along the border.

The increasing militarization of the border resulted in control and enforcement initiatives such as Operation Hold-the-Line (originally called Operation Blockade) and Operation Gatekeeper, which helped politicians dissipate the notion among their constituents that they were less than firm on immigration and that the country had lost control of its southern border.[100] The highly publicized rise in the number of apprehensions and deportations as a result of these undertakings nevertheless ignored the fact that clandestine immigration continued to rise, including of the kind border security measures are manifestly unsuitable to address, i.e., visa overstays. In fact, as much as half of the total number of illegal residents gained that status upon entering the United States with a valid non-immigrant visa and subsequently remaining in the country beyond the deadline the document established for their departure.[101]

In contrast, workplace regulation remained neglected throughout the first half of the 1990s. By 1999, only 2% of the INS budget was devoted to the inspection of employers of immigrant labor, which corresponded to roughly "340 full-time INS staffers detailed

---

99. Henderson, Beyond Borders, 130.

100. In Hopes and Prospects, Noam Chomsky observes that the militarization of the border began more effectively with Operation Gatekeeper launched during the administration of Bill Clinton, the same president who signed a "free-trade" agreement that nevertheless ignores Adam Smith's maxim that "'free circulation of labor is a foundation stone of free trade" (Chomsky, Noam. Hopes and Prospects. Penguin Books, 2011, 29).

101. Henderson, Beyond Borders, 131.

to inspect every job site in the United States."[102] By the same token, the Departments of Labor and Justice saw their budgets reduced during the Reagan and Bush administrations, defunding which signified the inadequate worksite enforcement of health and safety regulations. As a consequence, for many small and medium size companies, the risk of legal repercussions punishing the hiring of undocumented workers was therefore lower than the tax-free incentive associated with its practice.

On one hand, the shortcomings of NAFTA and the general state of disarray of the Mexican economy embodied push factors spurring northbound immigration; on the other, lax labor laws and the obvious demand for foreign laborers in the U.S. exerted a pull many underprivileged Mexicans were not in position to resist.

In the meantime, elevated levels of surveillance along the most historically popular stretches of border made stealthily crossing more difficult and dangerous. Consequently, *coyotage* fees rose considerably as their operations became more sophisticated and professionalized. More importantly, and as it had happened in 1986, these developments removed the natural incentive undocumented migrants already in the country had to return to Mexico for fear of not being able to come back across after a sojourn in the homeland. This effectively transformed a circular type of migration into more permanent immigration. Moreover, many parents who left their children to the care of relatives in Mexico now felt a greater inclination to reunite with their offspring in the U.S. since they were no longer able to easily travel across the border from Mexico after visiting with them during holidays or whenever there was an opportunity. The reinforcement of border security, namely of specific points of entry, and its deflection effect also resulted in the dispersion of prospective clandestine crossers along the international line in search for

102. Henderson, Beyond Borders, 125.

alternative entranceways into the United States. Thus, the settlement of new immigrants was driven to a degree of dispersion not seen before.

Illegal Immigration Reform & Immigrant Responsibility Act of 1996

The IIRAIRA was the culmination of a legislative process initiated shortly after the mid-term elections of 1994 resulted in the Republican party holding majorities in both the Senate and the House of Representatives. Among several provisions covering different issues distributed over six titles, the Act established sanctions for employers failing to comply with new regulations governing the hiring of immigrants. Border control was also strengthened, as new and heavier criminal sanctions were imposed on the use of counterfeit documentation, racketeering, and human smuggling inasmuch as these were related to immigration. The Border Patrol also saw its funding increased for the adoption of new monitoring and detection technologies; and for the hiring of even more agents— whose numbers would reach 12,200 by the end of the decade from a mere 2,000 in 1986.[103]

As vigilance at the border tightened by virtue of the multi-year enforcement plan called Operation Rio Grande,[104] successful surreptitious crossing demanded resorting to less impervious but more treacherous and unforgiving terrain, making the endeavor, although

---

103. Henderson, Beyond Borders, 144.

104. Beginning in the summer of 1997 in the Brownsville-Matamoros corridor and progressively extended to other areas following the border upstream the river that inspired its name, Operation Rio Grande dramatically increased the level of surveillance along the international boundary through the deployment of a momentous upsurge in manpower and equipment such as all-terrain vehicles, helicopters, surveillance cameras, motion sensors, x-ray machines, and canine units.

not impossible, significantly more perilous. As a result, the number of deaths associated with attempts to cross the border soared from 87 registered in 1996 to 499 recorded just four years later.[105] The most common causes of these fatalities were dehydration, hypothermia, and drug-trafficking-related violence inflicted on crossers while they attempted to navigate large stretches of desert in Texas, New Mexico, and Arizona. To add insult to injury, the increasingly higher level of resources required to run cross-border smuggling operations progressively facilitated the concentration of the business in the hands of a few and too often unscrupulous profiteers who preyed on the defenseless and vulnerable trekkers.

The effective militarization of the border and the vastly expanded role of detention and also streamlined deportation procedures for "excludable and deportable aliens" as a means to deal with unauthorized noncitizens had grievous consequences. Not only did it push immigrants illegally in the United States towards the clandestine fringes of society, it also encouraged them to remain in the country for much longer periods of time, often even permanently.

CAFTA

The 2005 Central America Free Trade Agreement is in essence an expansion of NAFTA to the five northernmost countries in Central America (Guatemala, Honduras, El Salvador, Nicaragua, and Costa Rica), as well as to the Dominican Republic.[106] As a product of a mindset based on the unfettered free market paradigm, the U.S.-sponsored CAFTA imposed on the treaty signatories policies

---

105. Henderson, Beyond Borders, 132.

106. Considering the geographic location of the Caribbean nation, the acronym was renamed CAFTA-DR after the Dominican Republic joined the negotiations in 2004. Unlike with NAFTA, Canada is not part of this agreement. The agreement became official in the United States after President George W. Bush signed it into law in 2005.

closely aligned with neoliberal doctrine. Embracing the holy trinity of neoconservatism thus meant 1) the privatization of large sectors of the economy previously controlled by the state, often at bargain prices and to foreign entities, who by nature are not committed as much to improving the services they provide to the citizens as they are to maximizing the profits their enterprises generate; 2) deregulation across the gamut of socioeconomic activity, chiefly among them those related to labor (including dismantling of labor unions) and to the environment, leading to the further erosion of workers' rights and protections and to the precipitous degradation of natural ecosystems, all in order to establish more business-friendly conditions so appealing to foreign investors; and 3) cutbacks, namely on social programs (not sparing education and healthcare) but also often on the level of taxation to the top tiers of the socioeconomic ladder.

As the provisions of the agreement were similar to that of NAFTA, so were its effects, acutely visible in the widening of the inequality gap and in the overall deterioration of the socioeconomic conditions at the lower social echelons of the United States and Mexico. The negative impacts of this and similar trade agreements are not so much deviations from a prescriptive norm; they are a result of structural imbalances between rich and poor nations, which have been proven to benefit the former at the expense of the latter whenever they interact. These asymmetries are heirs of a long colonial and neocolonial experience that by nature "perverts the economy of the colonies to its own ends, drains their wealth into the coffers of the metropolitan country and leaves them at independence with a large labour force and no capital with which to make that labour productive," as A. Sivanandan pointedly articulates.[107] It is therefore worth exploring, however succinctly, the origins of such inequalities, namely the ones that go beyond the obvious disparities in the scale

---

107. qtd. in Wellman and Cole 216.

of the respective markets and which remain instrumental in maintaining a status quo of eviscerating poverty in the most economically ravaged Central American nations.

Nicaragua

The rapacious legacy of the colonial era was not effaced with the creation of the United Provinces of Central America in 1823.[108] Intent on conquering all of Central America, the infamous Tennessee-born William Walker became the most notorious filibuster, wreaking havoc in the region during the 1850s after leading a group of mercenaries to capture Granada, then the capital of Nicaragua, and appointing himself president of the country. Once in power and in control of the regular army, Walker proceeded to not only legalize slavery, he also declared English the official language of the country, which is symbolic of his imperialist disposition and a foreshadowing of the Roosevelt Corollary of 1904.[109] Just a few years later, in 1912, U.S. Marines staged an intervention in Nicaragua to protect American business assets in the country as well as to prop up the regime of Adolfo Díaz, which had proven supportive of those same interests. The resistance to the U.S. occupation was led by Augusto

108. Upon gaining independence from Spain in 1821, the República Federal de Centroamérica was born. By 1840 the region had broken up into the modern states of Guatemala, El Salvador, Honduras, Nicaragua, and Costa Rica.

109. The Roosevelt Corollary to the Monroe Doctrine was articulated by President Theodore Roosevelt in his State of the Union address in 1904. In essence, Roosevelt enhanced the Monroe Doctrine (which curtailed the influence and interference of European powers in states and territories in the Western Hemisphere) by reserving the right of the United States to intervene in the affairs of any Latin American country whose default on their international financial obligations would invite retaliatory foreign military aggression. In practice, Roosevelt's "Big Stick" policy served as justification to a series of unilateral military interventions in various Central American and Caribbean nations throughout the rest of the century.

César Sandino, who became the main reason for the return of the Marines to the country fifteen years later, in 1927.[110] Anastasio Somoza was the ally of choice this time around, a dictator who, under the auspices of the United States, ordered the murder of Sandino and established a rule of terror and oppression for decades to come. After Anastasio's assassination in 1956, his sons Luis and Anastasio Jr. extended the corrupt Somoza dynasty, always with the reliable backing of the United States until 1979, when the Sandinista National Liberation Front ousted the regime.[111]

For over forty years, U.S.-based multinational corporations had benefited from a business environment favorable to their neocolonial designs, at the expense of the exploited workers whose rights were disregarded with systemic impunity. Over the years, the Somozas sent thousands of men to the United States to be trained in an array of military programs, training which would then be used to maintain the status quo of the reigning oligarchy by violent means while eliminating any opposition.

When the Sandinistas came to power in 1979, they initiated a series of socialist-leaning economic reforms and social programs aimed at reducing inequality and restoring social justice. These developments eventually gave rise to the infamous scheme that came to be known as the Iran-Contra affair. In short, in lieu of direct military intervention, the Reagan administration bypassed Congress and established a secret arrangement in which the proceedings of illegal armament sales to Iran (at the time at war with Iraq, a U.S. ally then) were diverted to fund paramilitary guerrilla groups in Nicaragua in their opposition to the Sandinista Junta of National Reconstruction. As a result, the country became a proxy battleground of the Cold

---

110. Booth, John A., et al. Understanding Central America: Global Forces, Rebellion, and Change. 6th ed., Westview Press, 2015, 99.
111. Booth 104.

War, taking the lives of at least 30,000 Nicaraguans and adding a full decade of frustrating prospects for progress and development in a nation that thus remained poor and an exporter of migrants.[112]

Guatemala

Sharing a similar historical legacy with Nicaragua, liberals and conservatives in independent Guatemala fought to fill the political vacuum left by Spain in 1821 into the middle of the 20th century. Late in the 19th century, President Justo Rufino Barrios was a catalyst for the modernization of the country by focusing on infrastructure and promoting foreign investment. Economic development came, however, on the heels of an increased concentration of landowner-ship, mostly for the cultivation of coffee, which quickly became the country's main crop and export. The Guatemalan government of-fered little to no protection to the peasants who forced out of their lands, which coffee growers controlled. Toward the end of the 19th century, a new factor came into play in Guatemala's agricultural landscape— the United Fruit Company. The U.S.-based corporation quickly drove local banana growers out of business and proceeded to accumulate vast portions of land, public utilities, and, inevitably, political influence. This model of development, where peasants and small farmers were forced to labor on mostly foreign-owned plan-tations under a system of debt peonage, continued under Manual Estrada Cabrera's even more brutal dictatorship and later under that of his successor, Jorge Ubico.

When Juan Arévalo became president in 1944, he initiated a se-ries of social and labor reforms, including nurturing workers' unions, to address the unrest that had been mounting since the years of the Great Depression and which had brought about a substantial de-cline in Guatemala's exports. But although the maldistribution of

---

112. Booth 107.

land, heir to persistent colonial ownership structures, was at the root of most socioeconomic problems, it was not to be addressed until Arévalo's successor, Jacobo Árbenz, was elected into office in 1951. Ambitious agrarian reform was among the many policies Árbenz proposed, mostly aimed at drawing economic power away from large landowners and employers to return it to peasants and workers. In this context, Árbenz set in motion a plan to swiftly expropriate the largest parcels of uncultivated land, most in the hands of agricultural conglomerates, by compensating their owners according to the value they had declared for tax purposes. This posed the most serious threat to the established oligopolies, who saw the hefty returns on their investment menaced. These large landowners were also displeased with the amount of compensations since the actual value of the land was much higher than they, in order to evade fair taxation, had actually claimed. Largely affected was one of such landowners, the aforementioned United Fruit Company, which in spite of lost favoritism in Guatemala still enjoyed plenty of clout in Washington, D.C. and, it turns out, Langley, VA.[113] What began with financial sanctions and diplomatic pressure intended on destabilizing Árbenz's administration soon expanded into disinformation actions and covert sabotage operations carried out by the CIA. Eventually, it led to the orchestration of a coup with the moral and material backing of the agency, promoting to power the main executioner of the plot, Colonel Castillo Armas.

---

113. Lars Schoultz acknowledges that Secretary of State John Foster Dulles had been partner in a law firm, Sullivan and Cromwell, with ties to United Fruit. His brother, Allen Dulles, was not only the director of the CIA, he was also a board member of United Fruit Company. Meanwhile, President Eisenhower's first Assistant Secretary of State for Latin America, John Moors Cabot, and the president of United Fruit Company, Thomas Dudley Cabot, were also brothers (Schoultz, Lars. Beneath the United States: a History of U.S. Policy toward Latin America. Harvard University, 1998, 337-38).

Armas set out to reverse all the reforms advanced by his predecessors, a process which entailed murdering and exiling thousands of those who opposed his deeds. Armas also set the tone for a political landscape dominated for years to come by the military elite at the service of wealthy landowners who had now regained control of most of the land, at the expense of peasants whose only alternative to toiling in the land was to move to slums in the cities. Peasant rebellions and public opposition was immediately quashed by police and military forces, usually under the command of officers trained at the School of the Americas at Fort Gulick and Fort Benning.[114]

The dependable and unconditional U.S. military backing of Guatemalan dictators over the decades eventually resulted in a civil war that showed its first signs as early as 1960, and which would last until 1996. The conflict claimed the lives of an estimated 200,000 Guatemalans in the period from 1978 to 1985 alone.[115] Many of those

114. The US Army School of the Americas (USARSA, or simply SOA) was first established in 1946 at Fort Gulick, in the Panama Canal Zone, under authority of the Department of War (renamed Department of Defense in 1949). It was relocated to Fort Benning, GA in 1984, maintaining the self-declared purpose of "providing military education and training to military personnel of Central and South American countries and Caribbean countries." The school, which also earned the moniker of "School of the Assassins" due to the less-than-professed nature of its teachings, trained 56,000 (64,000 by some accounts) military and police personnel from 22 countries until 2000— when it closed under the pressure of allegations of human rights abuses perpetrated by its graduates throughout the continent (US Army School). It reopened in 2001, in the same location and presumably with a similar mission, as the newly created "Western Hemisphere Institute for Security Cooperation" (WHINSEC). As of January 2018, it claims on its website to have trained over 24,000 students, military and civilian, originating in 36 different countries.
115. Booth 180. General Efraín Ríos Montt, for whom President Reagan expressed admiration as "a man of great personal integrity and commitment," stood out as one of the most murderous dictators of the 1980s. Trained at the School of the Americas in the Panama Canal Zone, he was the leader of the

who survived and were displaced by the war live today in the United States, home to about 1.5 million Guatemalans, representing 10% of the total population of Guatemala.[116] The large majority of their countrymen living back home continue to endure persistent poverty and thus easily find the motivation to leave the country.

El Salvador

When European chemical dyes slashed the demand for Salvadoran indigo dye and undercut the country's main economic activity by mid-19th century, El Salvador's economic elite began coveting the volcanic, higher-altitude farmland for the cultivation of the emerging cash crop of the day, coffee. As this elite class controlled the government, they initiated a process of "legal" appropriation of those lands which a population of mostly indigenous and mestizos had occupied after the Spanish had taken over their farmland on the fertile plains and valleys below. Before communal land holdings were outlawed altogether and in addition to vagrancy laws aimed at forcing peasants to work on plantations, capricious decrees made it difficult for small landowners and farmers to keep possession of their land, which would then become property of the agricultural oligarchy pushing for such legislation. This resulted in some of the most unequal distribution of land in all of Latin America, as the cultivation of coffee expanded unwaveringly, often at the expense of subsistence crops such as maize, rice, and beans— all staple elements in the diet of the Central American peoples. With the Great Depression and its global effects, including the collapse of the coffee

---

Guatemalan military junta that ruled the country between 1982 and 1983, period during which his deeds eventually granted him a conviction for genocide and crimes against humanity.
116. Dickinson, Eliot. *Globalization and Migration: a World in Motion.* Rowman Et Littlefield, 2017, 68.

market, agro businesses tried to recuperate some of their lost profits by cutting the already scant wages of their employees, giving rise to peasant uprisings promptly crushed by successive dictatorships consistently allied with the landed gentry.[117] For decades, the landowning elite continued to see their idiosyncratic interests safeguarded during alternating political cycles, often interrupted by coups, insofar as corruption and cronyism were common denominators to governments originating therefrom.

In the 1960s, reforms and plans for the modernization of the country produced substantial economic growth, although the concentration of investment and profits created an equally concentrated accumulation of wealth. Economic gains persisted being unevenly distributed during the years of the Central American Common Market.[118] The precursor to CAFTA failed to create the jobs and generate the trickle-down prosperity it promised, despite the rapid industrialization it facilitated, especially in El Salvador. A telling statistic of such disconnect is the growth of the country's industrial output, which doubled in the period between the mid-sixties and the mid-seventies, in spite of the sharp decrease in the number of companies responsible for such gained productivity. Meanwhile, the rural exodus caused by the deterioration of socioeconomic conditions in the countryside aggravated joblessness in urban and industrial centers. This dislocation exacerbated the already declining living conditions endured by the general population, giving rise to

---

117. In one of the most infamous instances, the massacre perpetrated by governmental forces on the western provinces of the country in 1932 passed through history as La Matanza. (The Slaughter). This ethnocide mounted to no less than the mass murder of an estimated 30,000 people (Booth 138).

118. In 1960, Guatemala, Honduras, El Salvador, Nicaragua, and, later (1962), Costa Rica formed the Mercado Común Centroamericano with the goal of integrating their economies in order to attain greater economic development for the region. The agreement came to an end in the mid-1980s.

intensified labor and social unrest both in the cities and the country. Meanwhile, a myriad of political parties, coalitions, and militant groups (including guerrillas) formed, signaling an unprecedented popular mobilization against the status quo. As in the past, social unrest was again met by violent repression. ORDEN[119] made a name for itself by murdering striking teachers, labor organizers, protesting peasants, or political opposition in general, not sparing clergy, an unfortunate recurrent pattern in the country's history. In 1974, for example, it was responsible for the assassination of Rafael Carranza, a labor organizer in the legislative opposition, in addition to the kidnapping and murder of numerous dissidents and social activists.

Because they were linked to the agrarian oligarchy, successive rightist presidents, all generals in the military, firmly opposed any reforms that could arguably lighten the social unrest and soothe the tense political atmosphere, recalcitrance which spawned a *coup d'état* in 1979. President Carter's administration quickly endorsed the new authority in El Salvador, a reform-minded government that was viewed as a way to avoid a civil war similar to that raging in neighboring Nicaragua. A new coalition government in El Salvador also meant that U.S. military aid to the country would resume after it had been briefly suspended following the rape and murder of four American missionaries by five members of the El Salvador National Guard in December of 1980.

---

119. ORDEN (Spanish for "Order"), the acronym for Organización Democrática Nacionalista (Nationalist Democratic Organization), was a staunchly anti-communist paramilitary counter-insurgency and vigilance organization founded in 1964. Its mission was to police the countryside and thwart any behavior it deemed suspect of being subversive. Indoctrination, intimidation, harassing and spying on insubmissive citizens were among the group's most benign activities. ORDEN "became increasingly active" after 1975, and "is just one example of US-sanctioned death squad activity throughout the Americas beginning in 1969." (Booth 143).

The most reactionary factions of the coalition swiftly prevailed over its reformist wing, however, which in practice meant the end of any hopes for actual reforms and a return to the business as usual political standing.

Also in 1980, various armed opposition groups joined forces to form the FMLN— *Farabundo Martí para la Liberación Nacional,* or Farabundo Martí Nacional Liberation Front. The Front was later endorsed by the FDR (*Frente Democrático Revolucionario,* or Revolutionary Democratic Front), a coalition of leftist parties in the opposition to the regime that lent political legitimacy and international recognition to the now FMLN-FDR. Established as a revolutionary powerhouse, the guerrilla force took control of some areas of the country and became well positioned to defeat the poorly organized Salvadoran armed forces and topple the military regime they defended. El Salvador was now officially in a state of civil war.

The newly inaugurated Reagan administration in Washington decisively changed the course of events that loomed large on El Salvador's political horizon. In 1981, military aid to the small Central American nation grew eightfold, and by 1984, El Salvador had become the third largest recipient of American aid in the world, behind only Israel and Egypt. This much boosted military assistance, in parallel with the U.S.-sanctioned refusal of a negotiated settlement, prolonged the conflict, as it helped the regular army hold off FMLN forces and perpetuate the state of terror among the civilian population for the rest of the decade. By the early 1980s, politically-related murders amounted to thousands and were a seemingly natural outcome of a general climate of torture and intimidation. Grim examples of the brutal ethos of the Salvadoran regime are the massacres perpetrated by the infamous Atlacatl Batallion, in addition to the widely publicized murders (albeit outside the realm of

American mainstream media[120]) of the outspoken Archbishop Oscar Romero in 1980, as well as that of six Jesuit priests in 1989.[121]

As the end of the Cold War made these proxy wars obsolete, the opposing factions finally negotiated peace in 1992. Subsequent investigations attributed 80% of the estimated 70,000 deaths, as well as 95% of human rights abuses during the civil war to police and armed forces.[122] To avoid fateful encounters with such forces, the number of Salvadorans migrating to the United States began skyrocketing in 1980, precisely around the time President Reagan justified support for wars in Central America as a way to prevent an upsurge of migrants entering the country. Instead, up to one-sixth of the Salvadoran population left their homeland since the beginning of the civil war, most to the United States, where an estimated 1.5 million lived by 2004.[123]

Successive conservative governments since the peace accords continued to embrace a neoliberal economic model whose policies typically disenfranchise large swaths of the population, leaving them

120. The disparities in U.S. media coverage of the political murders in El Salvador in comparison to similar coeval events elsewhere are exposed in detail in Herman, Edward S., and Chomsky, Noam. Manufacturing consent: The Political Economy of the Mass Media. New York: Pantheon Books, 2002.

121. The Atlacatl Battalion was a counter-insurgency military unit of the Salvadoran army that had been trained in the School of the Americas in the Panama Canal Zone. They were responsible for the El Mozote Massacre, in which as many as 900 men, women, and children suspected of sympathizing with the FMLN were murdered in the village whose name became forever associated with the bloodshed that occurred there on December 10, 1981. Later, in August of 1982, the same group staged an offensive in the central region of the country that resulted in the torture and death of more than 200 people, including children and elders. The infamous slaughter became known as El Calabozo Massacre. The unit was not disbanded until 1992, under the peace accords that ended 12 years of civil war.

122. Booth 150.

123. Booth 155.

no other recourse than to emigrate. The forced migration north inevitably produced the breakup of many family units whose youngsters then began gravitating towards gangs, both at home and in the host country. Members of the notorious MS-13 who were caught and deported back to El Salvador in the 1990s found fertile ground back home to reproduce the delinquency learned abroad, creating a vicious circle of violence-caused migration with no end in sight.

In spite of municipal and parliamentary electoral gains, the FMLN failed for a long time to capitalize its popularity in successful presidential bids. When the opposition group's candidate in the 2004 elections, Schafik Handal, declared an anti-CAFTA platform, it incurred in the wrath of the Bush administration, which proceeded to interfere in the electoral process by threatening retaliatory economic measures, such as those affecting remittances to the country, against El Salvador in case the "communist" candidate won..[124] The victory of a FMLN candidate would not materialize until 2009, when Mauricio Funes secured the election despite the renewed vitriolic Cold War rhetoric, this time around with war-on-terror undertones, encouraged by external meddling agents to the north.[125]

Notwithstanding their best efforts to curb violence and tackle poverty, neither Funes' nor subsequent administrations have succeeded in solving the problems of a deeply polarized society, one that remains hostage to grievous structural socioeconomic flaws

---

124. By 2008, remittances to El Salvador surpassed 3.8 billion dollars, representing a huge share of the country's GDP and by far the largest source of foreign currency (Booth 156).

125. California Republican Congressman Dana Rohrabacher associated the FMLN party with terrorism, equating it to Iran and Al-Qaeda, as well as claiming the organization was behind arms trafficking to Colombia. He also renewed threats he made in 2004 of termination of temporary protected status for Salvadorans residing in the United States, as well as of reconsidering remittance policies to El Salvador.

that have plagued the country for decades and which continue to encourage its most vulnerable citizens to seek greener pastures abroad.

Honduras

Unlike its closest neighbors, Honduras did not develop a significant export economy, and therefore failed to generate a wealthy mercantile class until much later, due in part to less favorable geographical and agricultural conditions. As a possible result, the country was also not the hotbed of rebellion against oligarchies as other nations in the region. Since coffee production and export in Honduras did not take off until after World War II, the emergence of a wealthy landowning coffee elite did not have as much time to materialize. Given the relative low quality of the land, even the prominent banana industry did not contribute to mass dislocation of peasants as early as in, for example, El Salvador. In fact, foreign-owned banana companies did not enjoy the same unconditional support from Honduran governments, and therefore the downward pressure on wages for workers in this less labor-intensive crop was not as consequential as elsewhere.[126] Nevertheless, shifting marketing conditions, a sudden surge in population, and the emergence of the Cold War mindset eventually prompted Honduras' history to converge with that of its closest neighbors by mid-20th century. As any signs of labor-related unrest were immediately labeled "communist," counteracting the "red threat" entailed the training of military personnel in the United States, as well as a significant increase in military aid from the same

---

126. Perhaps because of the lack of stauncher local support for its global corporate interests, several U.S. military incursions in the country occurred, during the first quarter of the 20th century, on behalf of the American fruit corporations that owned most of the land— fact which inspired the term "Banana Republics."

origin. Both factors contributed to the precipitous militarization of the country's political apparatus in the name of "national security."[127]

As a result of a coup in 1956, military governments became a constant well into the 1980s. The power of the military command also increased in direct proportion to the lavish military assistance provided by the Reagan administration. Such generosity was attributed as compensation for Honduras' logistic cooperation with the heavy presence of U.S. armed forces in its territory engaged in counterinsurgency operations against revolutionary forces in Nicaragua and El Salvador.[128] Although upheavals were not quashed as diligently and brutally as the sinister norm elsewhere in the isthmus, the U.S.-funded and trained Honduran military did not exempt itself from committing human rights abuses, such as the one that became known as the Los Horcones massacre.[129]

By the end of the 1980s, the United States lost interest in Honduras after the takeover by the Sandinistas in Nicaragua and the end of the Cold War, which meant a significant decrease in financial

---

127. Booth 211.

128. The United States military relied on Honduran territory to such an extent, and its influence on that nation was so pervasive that the country was referred to as "U.S.S. Honduras" or "Pentagon Republic" in some circles. Moreover, the presence of Salvadoran governmental forces and that of Nicaraguan Contras on Honduran soil with the purpose of receiving training from their American allies gave rise to diplomatic quarrels and political instability that resulted in the emergence of death squads and political murders/disappearances— atrocities to which Honduras had been immune until then. This in turn fomented the growth of leftist guerrillas in the country, although they remained relatively incipient.

129. In 1975, 15 religious figures (including two foreign priests, one from Colombia and the other from the United States), peasants, and student activists were murdered by Honduran armed forces in the vicinity of a ranch called Los Horcones. The perpetrators of the slayings were eventually prosecuted and convicted for their participation in the murders, but were later awarded amnesty, after serving as little as one year in prison.

assistance to the former. Nevertheless, the coercive shadow of the military autocracy loomed in the background well after the return of formal control of the government to civilians in 1982.

While using Honduras as a U.S. military subsidiary in Central America, the Reagan administration also left its indelible mark on the country's economic structure, namely by vigorously urging reforms predicated on deregulation, slashing funding for social programs, and focusing on the production of manufactured goods for export. In addition to destabilizing the coffee trade, this push towards industrialization disrupted traditional forms of agriculture in Honduras, ultimately resulting in a marked increase of Honduran emigration to the United States in the 1990s.[130]

The neoliberal reforms successive governments insisted on pursuing throughout the 1990s caused rampant poverty in the countryside. In the meantime, conditions in the cities further deteriorated as the rural exodus added to the stresses caused by overpopulation, which a weakened social safety net and infrastructure proved inadequate to address. Scarcity and overpopulation tend to coalesce into violence, and so gang activity in the country began reaching worrisome levels.

To make matters worse, Hurricane Mitch in 1998 hit Honduras harder than any other country, killing 11,000 people and exacerbating the already grinding poverty.[131] As the free-market orthodoxy left the country with scant financial resources to dedicate to social programs, unemployment and hardship rose sharply after the devastating storm, further buoying migration north. In *The Shock*

---

130. Nevins, Joseph. "How US policy in Honduras set the stage for today's migration." The Conversation, The Conversation US, Inc., 31 October 2016, theconversation.com/how-us-policy-in-honduras-set-the-stage-for-todays-migration-65935 (accessed January 17, 2019).
131. Booth 220.

Doctrine, Naomi Klein describes how, in addition to great material and human loss, further outcomes of the storm were a feverish privatization of all sorts of publicly held enterprises related to telecommunications, transportation, energy, and water.[132] In the same vein, the Honduran congress also "overturned progressive land-reform laws, making it far easier for foreigners to buy and sell property, and rammed through a radically pro-business mining law (drafted by industry) that lowered environmental standards and made it easier to evict people from homes that stood in the way of new mines."[133] The negative impact of these measures on the social tissue of Honduran society is easy to deduce: homelessness, poverty, delinquency, and anything else associated with lower living standards.

The legacy of a militaristic culture in governance surfaced again as recently as 2009, when President Manuel Zelaya, who had been advancing a rather progressive agenda, was overthrown by the military with support from the country's oligarchy and with the veiled endorsement of the U.S. State Department.[134] Although decrying Zelaya's ouster, the Obama administration acted as if actually supported the coup, namely by showing less interest in the reinstatement of the president elected in 2006 than in legitimizing the government resulting therefrom, contrary to the demands of the Organization of American States. Governmental corruption, fraud, runaway inequality, and violence in ever greater amounts ensued on the heels of an increasingly unfettered form of free-market economy embraced

---

132. Klein, Naomi. The Shock Doctrine: The Rise of Disaster Capitalism. New York: Metropolitan Books/Henry Holt, 2007, 395.

133. Klein 395.

134. After raising the minimum wage, Zelaya took steps to change the constitution of the country, which had been written under military control of the government. This bold move proved to cause angst among the economic elites and the military itself, which led to the overthrowing of the democratically-elected president.

by successive post-coup governments. The combination of eroding welfare and healthcare systems, a decrease on investment in education, the deregulation of labor, and growing violence on the streets continues to contribute to the mounting pressure on a large swath of the population to leave the country. Many have no other choice than joining northbound migration into the United States.

In summary, rather than mitigating the severe structural economic frailties of these ravaged nations, CAFTA is actually aggravating them, increasing poverty and inequality across the region, in a process displaying minor differences in degree from country to country, but similar in nature to all. As the borders are open to the free movement of goods and especially capital, the same freedom is not allowed to the citizens of these countries who are forced to stay and endure the adverse effects of these policies, even more so in conditions of a much-weakened social safety net. As with NAFTA, large American and often highly-subsidized agribusinesses flood Central American markets with grains at a price against which local smaller producers are unable to compete. This lopsided competition results in the extinction of businesses and jobs and leads to inevitable mass human displacement in these traditionally rural societies. In the meantime, similar imbalances are being produced in other sectors of these economies, which instead of translating into lower consumer prices rather culminate in lower wages, joblessness, and the depredation of the environment. Eventually, gang violence becomes rampant and the only option to escape insecurity and impoverishment is to emigrate north. It is thus no coincidence that these Central American countries are, after Mexico, the larger "exporter" of migrants to the United States. The recent surge in the numbers of minors attempting to reach the United Sates clandestinely is a telling reflex of the connection between pandemic gang violence in Central

America and massive migration therefrom. As Dickinson notes, "in 2011, U.S. authorities apprehended 15,949 unaccompanied children at the Mexico-U.S. border, and in 2014 that number had ballooned to 68,551. Nearly all come from El Salvador, Guatemala, Honduras— known as the Northern Triangle— and Mexico, and are fleeing various forms of poverty, mistreatment, and gang violence."[135]

9/11

During the first few months of the presidency of George W. Bush, which coincided with the dawn of Vicente Fox as the president of Mexico, there were encouraging signs of cooperation between the two heads of state, presaging a much-needed bi-lateral immigration reform for the new millennium. Both presidents displayed receptiveness to endorsing a guest-worker program that helped simplify the issuance of visas to Mexican migrants. Additionally, President George Bush did not obviously opposed supporting the formulation of a path to legal residency to those living in the United States illegally.

The terrorist attacks of September 11, 2001, in New York and Washington utterly changed the mindset of the political establishment in the United States, insofar as national security anxieties and inflated sensitivity to external threats shifted the course of both domestic and foreign policy towards unilateralism. This shift entailed a renewed and even more vigorous focus on border control and on eradicating illegal immigration. The Patriot Act, for example, included provisions to streamline the deportation of undocumented immigrants without a hearing, so long as there were suspicions of terrorist activity.[136]

---

135. Dickinson 56.

136. The full title of the Act is "Uniting and Strengthening America by Providing Appropriate Tools Required to Intercept and Obstruct Terrorism Act of

Later, in November of 2005, and following the creation of the Department of Homeland Security, its Secretary Michael Chertoff announced the Secure Border Initiative. The five-year plan pledged to increase border infrastructure (meaning physical barriers and detection technology), expand detention facilities (both in number and in size), and grow the ranks of border patrol agents, criminal investigators, fugitive operations teams, immigration enforcement agents, and deportation officers.[137]

About a month later, Congress entertained the idea of enacting a legislative measure tentatively titled "Border Protection, Anti-terrorism, and Illegal Immigration Control Act." Even though the bill did not pass the Senate, the label attached to the document, let alone its draconian provisions, had the merit of exposing the gloomy legislative ethos of its advocates, for it contributed to the conflation of immigrants— legal and illegal alike— with terrorists and criminals in the collective consciousness of the nation. The bill, HR4437, was introduced by congressman James Sensenbrenner and proposed to regard all twelve million undocumented immigrants in the United States as federal criminals, along with anyone who directly or indirectly assisted them in their masquerade— including teachers, medical personnel, and religious clerics. Incidentally, it also recommended the erection of a 700-mile wall along the southern border, an idea that recently resurfaced in political minds. The following year, George W. Bush proved that defeating the bill stopped neither the isolationist impulses nor the wall-building frenzy; the Secure Fence Act of 2006 ordered the construction of new, as well as the reinforcement of existing fencing along the southern border, thus adding to the already colossal budget assigned to border surveillance. In

---

2001"— more commonly known by its ten-letter abbreviation "USA PATRIOT" or simply "Patriot Act."
137. Henderson, Beyond Borders, 142-43.

fact, funding for Border Patrol increased 146% under Bush's 2000-2008 mandate, while the number of agents on the ground nearly doubled.[138]

The effects of the Secure Border Initiative were soon felt in the form of a series of military-style raids carried out by ICE (Immigration and Customs Enforcement) in 2006.[139] The apprehension and removal of individuals from their homes and places of employment caused considerable disruption of families and businesses, yet very few people faced prosecution following these initiatives for illegal hiring of undocumented immigrants. As with wall-building, a cost/benefit analysis of this type of anti-immigration action proves to be a tremendous waste of money, although they are very effective in growing rather than easing social, political, and economic anxieties associated with immigration. In concert with the uneasiness displayed by the federal government towards illegal immigration, dozens of nativist civil militia groups were by these days taking matters into their own hands and performing acts of vigilance and enforcement along the border and beyond.[140]

The economic downturn beginning in 2008 that developed into the Great Recession, as well as the unprecedented surge of drug-related violence at the border, proved to be far more effective at curtailing the flow of illegal immigrants from Mexico than any government

---

138. Orrenius, Pia M., and Madeline Zavodny. Beside the Golden Door: U.S. Immigration Reform in a New Era of Globalization. Washington, D.C.: AEI, 2010, 35.

139. "The Cost of Immigration Enforcement and Border Security." American Immigration Council, American Immigration Council, 25 January 2017, americanimmigrationcouncil.org/research/the-cost-of-immigration-enforcement-and-border-security (accessed May 15, 2018). According to the American Immigration Council, "the number of ICE agents devoted to its office of Enforcement and Removal Operations (ERO) nearly tripled from FY 2003 to FY 2016."

140. Henderson, Beyond Borders, 145.

policies and civil acts of vigilantism aiming at its restriction. But if the stricter border build-up and enforcement fall short of justifying the reduction of the illicit trickle of immigrants across the international line during a period of economic contraction, it may explain why few of the estimated millions of Mexicans living in the United States illegally opted to return to Mexico in a period of manifest scarcity of employment opportunities.

As immigration control mechanisms were streamlined, caught in the deportation dragnet were youngsters who were brought into the United States as small children and who had grown up in an environment of urban delinquency, especially in the Los Angeles area. As a result, "US deportations of Central Americans with criminal records pushed populations of decultured members of US urban gangs into several countries in Central America," who then proceeded to wreak havoc on the already deficient social and economic infrastructure of nations recently battered by civil wars and facing economic collapse.[141] Because of the abundant remnants of said civil wars there was no shortage of weaponry to be found among the civil society, which provided the perfect conditions for the breeding of transnational gang violence. The environment of extreme insecurity among the populations of these countries forced them to seek alternatives to escape the now widespread social turbulence, many of them seeing migrating north as the only viable alternative. It is of no little irony that in addition to the sponsoring of political and economic volatility throughout Central America, it is also the deportation policies of the United States that end up feeding the fluxes of undocumented migration into the country. Unfortunately, many escape almost-certain death at home to perish thousands of miles away along the U.S.-Mexico border. According to an August, 2006, United States Government Accountability Office report, the

---

141. Booth 44.

number of border-crossing deaths doubled in the ten years between 1995 and the peak year of 2005 to a total of about 4,000. In turn, the Washington Office on Latin America points out that 2012 comes at a close second— registering 463 deaths, even though the number of attempts to make such cross was significantly lower in 2012 than in it had been in 2005.[142] This can only mean crossing the border has become more dangerous and deadly, in direct correlation to the heightened number and level of sophistication of mechanisms of control in place. Moreover, fewer migrants seemed to originate from Mexico than from Central American countries.

The "War on Drugs"

While the efforts to curb so-called communist impulses subsided and resources were diverted, especially after 9/11, toward combating international terrorism, in Latin America it's the "war on drugs" that continues to attract U.S. attention and secure funding therefrom. This financial assistance, mostly military in nature, also persists in driving sovereign nations to relinquish their self-determination to policies dictated by Washington, usually with disastrous social-economic consequences.[143] Military assistance effectively "re-militarizes"

---

142. Isacson, Adam and Meyer, Maureen. "The Alarming Rise of Migrant Deaths on U.S. Soil— And What to Do About It." WOLA: Advocacy for Human Rights in the Americas, Washington Office on Latin America, 24 April 2013, wola.org/analysis/the-alarming-rise-of-migrant-deaths-on-us-soil-and-what-to-do-about-it (accessed March 19, 2019).

143. According to NACLA Reports on the Americas, yearly military contract funds to Latin America and the Caribbean rose from an average of $121 million in 2001 to $438 million by 2010 (Lindsay-Poland, John. "Beyond the Drug War: The Pentagon's Other Operations in Latin America." NACLA Report on the Americas, vol. 44, no. 3, May 2011, 8). On the other hand, direct counter-narcotics funding to Mexico doubled in 2009 to $830 million (Reiss, Suzanna. "Beyond Supply and Demand: Obama's Drug Wars in Latin America." NACLA Report on the Americas, vol. 43, no. 1, Jan. 2010, 27).

these countries, particularly those ravaged by decades of military authoritarianism in Central America, meaning that "national militaries are deployed for policing, with disastrous consequences for human rights."[144]

Abroad as at home, containing the scourge of narcotics has meant focusing almost exclusively on the supply-side of the phenomenon, which implies a commitment to strengthen the coercive mechanisms at the disposal of the respective governments. This results not only in the inordinate militarization of police agencies, but it also bolsters the involvement of the armed forces in domestic civilian affairs. By criminalizing drug users, this punitive approach has also contributed to the steep increase of prison populations in step with the escalation of poverty in these militarized societies. Instead of curbing drug production and trafficking, the repressive model has only aggravated violence and insecurity in the midst of these societies, as criminal organizations are further economically strengthened by the soaring drug street prices which suppressive measures bolster. Violence between rival groups is as rampant as the corruption of public officials, both in Mexico and in the Northern Triangle (Guatemala, Honduras, El Salvador), often in overt defiance of the security forces, thus making a mockery of the judicial systems in these countries. Even more grievous than severely undermining democracies, this subversion of the rule of law often tramples on the human rights of an already impoverished population. Instead of devoted to guaranteeing their safety, many Latin-Americans see the power of the state (mis)used to muffle dissenting political voices through intimidation or to clamp down on the least acquiescent citizens.

In addition to the adverse effects of the purportedly well-intentioned policies sponsored, funded, and often coordinated by the U.S.

---

144. Farthing, Linda. "The Time to Finally Stop the 'War on Drugs' Is Now." NACLA Report on the Americas, vol. 48, no. 4, Winter. 2006, 320-21.

government, other factors emanating from the United States have enabled the generalized violence these societies face. One is the obvious fact that the relentless demand for psychotropic substances in the United States (and in Europe) creates a market for them, thus sustaining a whole industry; the other, equally sinister, is the easy access to high-caliber weapons permissive gun laws in the Unites States allow. As a result, and according to Reiss reporting for NACLA, most of the guns behind the violence in Mexico and Central America originate in the United States, where they are easily purchased.[145]

Indigenous communities have borne the heaviest burden of the collateral damage these policies inflict. Coca plantation eradication campaigns in the countryside have served as justification for the use of chemicals that cause lasting contamination of the soil, making it unusable for any future crop. The pretext does not spare traditional livelihoods in the Andes region, where poor farmers see their traditional coca crops outlawed and are left without alternatives to their subsistence. In his book titled *Who Rules the World*, Chomsky goes as far as correlating the process of fumigation to "chemical warfare," referring to the particular case of Colombia.[146] Whether as part of a wider scheme to subdue and exterminate large swaths of its indigenous population, as the same author suggests, its demographic effects are undeniable— peasants flee rural areas in massive numbers, heading towards urban slums. Reiss observes that Colombia and Mexico suffer the most severe consequences of this state of affairs, where "drug war failures" result in "thousands of displaced peoples, environmental devastation, and documented human rights

---

145. Reiss, Suzanna. "Beyond Supply and Demand: Obama's Drug Wars in Latin America." NACLA Report on the Americas, vol. 43, no. 1, Jan. 2010, 30.
146. Chomsky, Noam. Who Rules the World? Metropolitan Books, 2016, 14.

abuses."[147] In turn, this dislocation brings misery and social unrest to the cities, deepening the socioeconomic desperation that eventually generates migrants and leads them north.

It is apparent that the prohibitionist and militaristic counter-narcotic approach to the drug problem falls short of eradicating it or even scaling it down— quite the contrary. Instead, it has both exacerbated existing problems and created new ones, all at the root of migration pressures that usually materialize in illegal immigration into the very country backing the failed repressive policies.

Dream Act and deferment policies

Even though the first few years of the Obama administration silently reversed the most confrontational anti-illegal immigration policies of the Bush era, the number of deportations soared to an all-time high during his presidency. On the other hand, both the President and a majority Democratic Congress exerted pressure to pass legislation that had been failing enactment throughout the decade: the Dream Act.[148] The bill, the first version of which had been introduced in Congress in 2001, would have established a conditional path to citizenship to underage children of illegal immigrants under certain circumstances. Upon failing to overcome a Republican filibuster in the Senate, the act was adopted, in a way, by a handful of states whose legislatures decided to allow in-state tuition to undocumented students. As the number of states with such legal provisions has increased over the years, so have the slight variations in the requirements dictated by each one. The common denominator is that the applicants must have graduated from their primary and secondary schools.

---

147. Reiss 30.
148. Acronym for "Development, Relief, and Education for Alien Minors."

At the federal level, and as a reaction to the failure of the bill to pass the Senate, the Obama administration instituted in 2012 a policy aiming at protecting certain undocumented persons who entered the country illegally as minors— a program known as DACA.[149] The program allows these minors to benefit from deferred action on deportation during renewable two-year periods, within which they are also eligible to receive a work permit. Unlike what was proposed with the Dream Act, the DACA program does not provide a path to citizenship to children who have not known any other homeland.

As of June, 2016, U.S. Citizenship and Immigration Services (US-CIS) had received about 845,000 requests from applicants seeking to benefit from the program, having approved about 88% of them. In the meantime, the Migration and Policy Institute estimates the total DACA-eligible population in the United States is 2.3 million.[150] The discrepancy between the figures can be justified by some of these individuals not being *immediately* eligible, either for not having yet reached the minimum application age and/or otherwise attained the minimum education level required by the program. It is also worth considering more prosaic factors such as the considerable expense associated with the application process— almost $500 currently, an unfeasible amount for many low-income families; or the understandable recalcitrance some undocumented families feel in disclosing personal information for fear that surrendering their anonymity will make them more vulnerable, and thus easy targets for deportation should the program be terminated in the future.

In 2014, the Obama administration sought to extend the principles of the DACA program to the undocumented parents of children

---

149. Acronym for "Deferred Action for Childhood Arrivals."
150. Gelatt, Julia. "More Than a DREAM (Act), Less Than a Promise." MPI— Migration Policy Institute, Migration Policy Institute, March 2019, migrationpolicy.org/news/more-dream-act-less-promise (accessed March 19, 2019).

born in the United States or who have become lawful permanent residents, an initiative known as DAPA.[151] The proposal faced lawsuits from several states claiming it violated the Constitution and therefore never went into effect.

Whether to appease the leanings of restrictionists, nativists, or immigration hard-liners in Congress, the whole of the legislative initiatives discussed above have in common the inclusion in their drafting of provisions centered on increasing border controls rather than on addressing the issues at the root of illegal immigration—namely by disregarding the pull and push factors underlying it. Moreover, the near impossibility of anyone originating from Mexico or Central America today to emigrate to the United States legally and in a timely manner is another idea deserving of more serious consideration.

As a result of this focus on the southern border, U.S. Customs and Border Protection (USCBP) is today the largest law enforcement agency in the United States, with a 2017 budget of $14 billion and staffed by about 60,000 employees, according to a budgetary overview published by the Department of Homeland Security.

Nevertheless, it seems apparent that border controls and enforcement have proven inefficient in curtailing illegal immigration from the south, which has rather fluctuated in consonance with economic cycles not only in Mexico (and, more recently, socioeconomic havoc in Central America) but also, and especially in the United States, where cheap illegal labor is seen as instrumental in periods of growth but easily turned to an expendable scapegoat in times of economic gloom. Cole makes this point clear by stating that "close

---

151. Acronym for "Deferred Action for Parental Accountability," but also known as "Deferred Action for Parents of Americans and Lawful Permanent Residents."

examination of the immigration regimes of liberal democratic societies states shows that they are designed around economic considerations, seeking immigrants who will meet their economic needs and rejecting those who do not."[152]

At the time of this writing, a much-heightened anti-illegal immigrant rhetoric once again dominates the political discourse, with the new administration's promises of grandiose wall-building and unrelenting crackdown on "illegal aliens." It seems obvious that we either do not learn much from history or prefer to ignore it altogether.

---

152. Wellman and Cole 196.

Part 2
Deportation policies and the criminalization of immigration

The contingency of one's nationality as largely determinant of one's fate is, from an ethical standpoint, a problematic notion.[153] This philosophical intricacy takes a moral turn when immigration policies that affect the lives of millions of individuals are discordant to the values extolled by the political class whenever its members deem convenient. The "toughness on immigration" can arguably be seen as both a cause and effect of social anxieties regarding the "other," because it highlights and accentuates the dichotomy between legal and illegal, between those who are entitled to full membership in the national club and those who are not, between basically those who are "like us," and those who are not, the latter viewed as a threat to the American cultural integrity. Deportation is, after rejection of admission at the border, the main tool used to exclude those who have been determined as not belonging and deserving of the privileges of citizenship— even in its broad, transnational sense. Among those affected by often capricious exclusion practices are the children of the deportees who, often, are American citizens by birthright. Citing a 2010 report published by the schools of law at the University of California, Berkeley and Davis, Daniel Kanstroom observes that

---

153. Christopher Wellman and Phillip Cole offer their confronting but dispassionate views on this subject in Debating the Ethics of Immigration: Is There a Right to Exclude? (Oxford University Press, 2011).

the deportation of an undocumented parent (out of the reported 108,000) impacted "nearly 88,000 U.S. citizen children" in the decade between 1997 and 2007.[154] Perhaps tellingly, the United States of America is the only country on earth that has yet to ratify the United Nations Convention on the Rights of the Child, a treaty that has been in effect in most of the world since 1990. This stance adds to statistics regarding the protection of children and their well-being, ranging from infant mortality to child poverty rates, that are not very flattering to the "greatest democracy on earth."

The problems associated with deportation of "excludable" individuals need to be analyzed not only within the broader context of a greatly militarized law enforcement system and the mass incarceration rates that characterize American society today, but also in terms of the less-than-stellar record regarding the rights of minorities transversal to arguably every aspect of the nation-building project since colonial times. In *Deportation Nation*, Kanstroom argues that the concept of deportation constitutes not only a "system of exclusion," but also a "tool of discretionary social control" and a "mechanism of scapegoating."[155] This more or less veiled legal device has been interwoven with the fluid concept of citizenship, something that has been subject of discussion among the intellectual and political elites since the times of the Roman Empire. In turn, it has been historically subordinated to social constructs such as "religion, wealth, health, and morality," going back as far as European feudal times. Ethnicity and political ideology were added later as criteria for "acceptance."[156] In fact, the United States as a so-called melting

---

154. Kanstroom, Dan. Aftermath: Deportation Law and the New American Diaspora. New York: Oxford U, 2014, 141.

155. Kanstroom, Dan. Deportation Nation: Outsiders in American History. Harvard Univ. Press, 2010, 5.

156. Kanstroom, Deportation Nation, 48.

pot and a nation of immigrants has, paradoxically, a rather extensive track record of preclusion of individuals and groups from full participatory status. From non-British foreigners to Loyalists, followed by southern and eastern Europeans, Native Americans and African slaves; from Asians and most recently to Latin Americans and Middle Easterners— they all have experienced their share of exclusion to any given degree and seemingly along ethnic lines, either by praxis or by ad hoc legislative devices. This paradox is emboldened when we think of Ellis Island both as the entry port for "huddled masses yearning to breathe free," and later as a detention and deportation center, a bitter irony not always present in the American collective memory.

The step from exclusion to expulsion was indeed not a long one, insofar as the current system of deportation may be seen as having its roots both in the forceful removal of Native Americans from their lands and in laws enacted to address fugitive and then freed African slaves.[157] While the former were pushed westward and coerced into surrendering their fertile lands to the Anglo-Americans, plans were developed for the "relocation" of the latter to Central America, Haiti, and even back to Africa. This led to the establishment of Liberia in 1848, a sovereign nation effectively founded on the basic principle of deportation. President Abraham Lincoln himself (as Thomas Jefferson before him, among others), convinced of the social incompatibility between ethnicities, proposed to Congress in 1862 that it allocate funding for "colonizing free colored persons, with their

---

157. Signed by President Andrew Jackson on May 28, 1830, the Indian Removal Act was a visible component of the systematic effort to usurp Native American land in the Southeast by relocating its rightful owners farther west against their will. For good reason, Howard Zinn refers to Andrew Jackson as "the most aggressive enemy of the Indians in early American history" (Zinn, Howard. A People's History of the United States. Harper Perennial, 2015, 127).

consent, at any place or places without the United States."[158] This mindset clearly underscores the racialized nature of the exclusion routines at the foundation of American immigration and deportation laws and accentuates a clear "us-versus-them" social and political dynamic. Likewise, laws aiming at the exclusion of "coolies" enacted by the California legislature in the Anti-Coolie Act of 1862 eventually prompted the exclusion of all Chinese laborers. The Chinese Exclusion Act of 1882, as mentioned above, marked the beginning of the establishment of interdiction mechanisms operating overtly on the basis of nationality. This was followed by the Gentleman's Agreement with Japan in 1907 and the Quota Laws of the 1920s. Stemming from a growing anti-Japanese nativist sentiment in California, the Roosevelt Administration informally agreed to not impose immigration restrictions on Japanese nationals, as long as Japan refrained from issuing passports to those citizens intending on immigrating to the continental United States— thus allowing Japan to avoid the humiliation to which China had been subjected with the Exclusion Act in 1882. The agreement was eventually annulled by the quotas imposed by the Immigration Act of 1924, which unilaterally barred the legal entry into the United States of all Asian immigrants, along with others deemed undesirable. Cole points that such quotas were "designed to restrict immigration from southern and eastern Europe, in favor of 'superior' northern and western Europeans."[159] Aviva Chomsky suggests that behind this type of legislation are Madison Grant's[160] theories, according to which "the most

---

158. qtd. in Kanstroom, Deportation Nation, 89.

159. Wellman and Cole 218. The same author adds that the quotas set by the 1924 Immigration Act "prevented the entry into the United States of perhaps six million southern, central and western Europeans" in the 1924-1939 period, many of "whom were to be murdered in the Nazi extermination program" (218).

160. Madison Grant (1865-1937) was a Yale graduate and a race theorist with

practical and hopeful method of race improvement is through the elimination of the least desirable elements of the nation by depriving them of the power to contribute to future generations."[161]

These laws included provisions that arguably prevail to this day within the inner workings of the legal system regarding immigration and deportation praxis. Considering the U.S. Constitution makes no reference to deportation nor does it bestow upon the federal government the power to regulate immigration matters, it quickly becomes apparent that immigration and deportation laws are in a category of their own. Consequently, they enjoy a status of extraconstitutional exceptionalism that often grants the agents in charge of their enactment and enforcement a degree of authority strangely exempt of judicial oversight. This exceptionalism markedly draws the line dividing citizens and noncitizens, even though the Constitution is equally omissive in regard to the rights of the latter as it falls short of clearly distinguishing between ones and others. The fact that the rights of "persons" have been interpreted to extend equal rights under the law to anyone irrespective of citizenship (in *sensu stricto*) further adds to this systemic anomaly. However, and as Noam Chomsky observes in *Occupy*, the courts of the land have had a pivotal role in changing the

---

strong beliefs regarding Nordic racial superiority. As a stalwart defender of the preservation of such ethnic heritage in North America, he advocated for exclusion, segregation, sterilization, and went as far as suggesting extermination of "racially inferior" peoples. Besides authoring influential books such as The Passing of the Great Race (1916), he was also one of the architects of the Immigration Restriction Act of 1924 mentioned above.

161. qtd. in Chomsky, Aviva. "They Take Our Jobs!": And 20 Other Myths about Immigration. Boston, MA: Beacon, 2007, 174. According to the same author, his acclaimed ideas "also provided scholarly justification for sterilization campaigns directed against citizens who were considered undesirable." These claims invite us, at the very least, to reconsider the narrative buttressing the commonly accepted notion of an altruistic nation built upon the magnanimous values of inclusiveness and democracy for all.

concept of "person" over the years. While they worked on "broaden it to include corporations," they "narrowed it to exclude undocumented immigrants."[162]

It is thus worth examining, however succinctly and in abstract, the unorthodox conditions from which formal immigration and deportation laws emerged. According again to Kanstroom, the first stride in that direction was the appropriation of immigration control by the federal government during the 1800s.[163] From a localized mechanism of exclusion of undesirables[164]— a category that roughly included poor, unhealthy, criminal, and morally deviant individuals— immigration matters became the realm of the federal government during the last decades of the 19th century. This shift was produced under the general assumption that immigration was an issue of the same order as international relations, and hence under the competence and authority of Washington's technocracy. Such rationale helped the central government detach immigration laws from the scope of the Constitution, which was deemed to be exclusively of domestic consequence. The exceptionalism of immigration law was thus unofficially instituted. [165]

A second necessary development to further consolidate bypassing constitutional protection by federal deportation laws was to legitimize them in the eyes of the public and the court system itself. Such legitimation came on the heels of the labor struggles that

---

162. Chomsky, Noam. Occupy. Penguin Books, 2012, 41.

163. Kanstroom, Deportation Nation, 93.

164. During the Revolutionary War and beyond, as before in medieval Europe, land ownership as a sine qua non for the granting of permission to individuals to reside in towns other than that of their birth was a well-established practice.

165. Howard Zinn observes that "the Constitution gave no right to Congress to deport aliens, but the Supreme Court had said, back in 1892, in affirming the right of Congress to exclude Chinese, that as a matter of self-preservation, this was a natural right of the government" (Zinn 375).

characterized the American landscape during the second half of the 19th century. Initially a West Coast phenomenon, the "problem" of Chinese immigration eventually gained national notoriety with the extreme demonization of Chinese laborers added to a much emphasized assertion of their purported racial inferiority versus the much superior and civilized Anglo-Americans. Not only were Chinese immigrants capriciously barred from obtaining U.S. naturalization, the citizenship of women who married Asian citizens was to be revoked, even after the Cable Act of 1922 protecting the American citizenship of women regardless of their marital status. This xenophobic ethos, which had in reality been part of the national mindset since the onset of colonial times in relation to other ethnicities and nationalities, including Europeans, sought further justification in the presumed high crime rates perpetrated by these immigrants as a clear sign of their depravity and unprincipled character. The "war on crime," whether legitimate or imaginary, became then an imperative, and with this narrative came the validation of harsh exclusion policies aiming at ridding American society from pernicious outside influences. The United States would finally lift its legal barriers to citizenship for most Asian immigrants on the onset of WWII as an incentive to their loyalty in the war effort against Japan.

Finally, the present state of deportation laws were generated by a third momentous ingredient: the extension of border control laws well beyond the vicinity of the nation's borders. This geographic expansion equates to a broadening conceptual approach to immigration law that suggests its exclusion penchant. As such, it renders deportation as a mechanism pertaining more to the notion of "not belonging" than that of mere border control.

This last factor has long been substantiated in concrete actions unsubtly aimed at the exclusion and expulsion of those deemed as not belonging in the national "club." The Palmer Raids, for example, sought to capture and deport leftists and anarchists suspected of subversive activities in the United States[166]— a proposition with a clear ideological base that nevertheless markedly encapsulates the social control vocation of deportation statutes and their enforcement.

In turn, the previously mentioned Operation Wetback, initiated in 1954 having started in the Rio Grande valley, soon made its way north and away from the border exclusively targeting undocumented Mexican laborers. This operation, the first of many carried out over the following decades with similar racialized undertones, displayed attributes and produced outcomes that abundantly illustrate some sinister aspects of deportation as a mechanism of social control. "Expedited removals" were thus no longer a border convention, but a rather predominant practice applied elsewhere to the same effect, and with similar deficient judicial oversight. This also reinforces the pragmatic view of immigration on the part of the authorities who, in cahoots with economic agents, conceived Mexicans as good laborers, but not good immigrants or potential citizens. It is not a coincidence that by the 1930s, the Department of Immigration was the largest of all Labor Department agencies. The historical proximity between labor and immigration legislation and praxis examined above are well illustrative of this dynamics.

Today, non-citizens in the United States may be deported at the whim of the federal government at any time and for any reason—including retroactively, i.e., for offenses that did not imply penalty of removal at the time of their commission. The unfortunate events of September 11, 2001, further exacerbated this capriciousness, as

---

166. This series of raids, named after Attorney General Alexander Mitchell Palmer, were conducted by the Department of Justice in the context of the Red Scare that followed the triumph of the Bolsheviks in Russia; and the subsequent commitment of a militarily victorious Soviet Union in spreading communist ideals internationally post-World War I.

deportation regulations were often used for clearly pretextual purposes, an overreach that had little to do with immigration and therefore outside of the realm of immigration law. The deportation threat
contributes to depressing wages (undocumented workers agree to
work for less), and immigration enforcement is also, even more au-
daciously, used as a weapon to curb union activity, as scrutinized by
David Bacon in his *Illegal People*.[167]

By the 1950s, criminalization of immigration (or "crimmigra-
tion") was a process in advanced stages of maturation, long before
the creation of the Alien Criminal Apprehension Program in the late
1980s. "The convergence of immigration and criminal law" as a factor weakening of immigrants' rights had a pivotal moment in 1940,
when the Bureau of Immigration and Naturalization was transferred
from the Department of Labor to the Department of Justice.[168] This
shift contributed to a decisive change of paradigm that framed immigration, albeit informally, as a criminal matter as opposed to a
civil one, which had been the prevalent notion in the earlier years of
the century. This also allowed the agency to benefit from substantial
increases in its budget, whose effects on border control have been
outlined above. Nevertheless, and in spite of the efforts of some lawmakers over the years to make unsupervised entry of non-U.S. citizens into the country a felony under federal criminal law, it currently represents simply a misdemeanor offense and thus carries minor

---

167. Although an examination of the benefits undocumented immigration
brings to the U.S. economy falls outside the scope of this work, it is worth
noting that the irregular status of immigrants mounts indeed to a situation of
"taxation without representation." Besides indirect taxes, many pay into Social
Security, namely when using fake (i.e. someone else's) social security numbers— without ever raking in the corresponding benefits.
168. Macías-Rojas, Patrisia. From Deportation to Prison: The Politics of Immigration Enforcement in Post-civil Rights America. New York: New York UP,
2016, 23.

civil penalties. The same can be said about unlawful presence in the country without proper documentation.

In practice, however, the civil penalties imposed on undocumented immigrants (fines and jail time) may, ultimately at the discretion of the Department of Homeland Security, swiftly devolve into criminal sanctions disproportional to those imposed on the native born for equivalent offenses, namely deportation. Given this legal schism between native and foreign born, the latter run a chronic risk of seeing their civil rights abridged and their cases falling outside the realm of constitutional due process.

Aside from these historical and philosophical considerations, a set of more recent law enforcement priorities, not always directly related to immigration, drew upon certain logistics that contributed to molding deportation standards to a considerable extent. The Comprehensive Crime Control Act of 1984, arguably the most relevant revision of the American criminal code of the century, set the wheels in motion for sizable collateral repercussions on the expanse of the deportation paradigm. The encouragement of mandatory minimum prison sentences, pre-trial detentions, and broadened forfeiture mechanisms (both locally and at the federal level) led to a substantial increase in the prison population, and with it a bed shortage that imposed an unprecedented strain on detention facilities across the country. While overcrowded federal detention facilities did not, at first, directly impact detained immigrants, since the INS subcontracted prison space for their exclusive use, they would nevertheless add to the overburdening of the country's incarceration infrastructure, as the immigration system had been engaging in mass detention of its own since 1981. The policy of non-detention embraced by the INS until then was abandoned in favor of an across the board mandatory detention policy of deportable migrants as a matter of principle. This shift came in the wake of the mass influx of

Cuban refugees generated by the Mariel boatlift of the year before, in addition to the large number of asylum seekers from Haiti, and also those fleeing from the civil wars that engulfed the northernmost Central American nations during the early 1980s. With prison capacities already pushed to the limit, the Anti-Drug Abuse Act of 1986 added insult to injury by reframing the approach to substance abuse from a rehabilitative to a punitive model; not only was mandatory detention made standard procedure in dealing with the problem, the Act also revised the typology of the offenses that would fall under such sanction.

Facing severe prison overcrowding from these measures, Congress sought to enact legal mechanisms that expanded and expedited criminal deportations of non-citizens, including for drug offenses charges, in order to release bed space in prisons for native born offenders. In this context, the INS established the aforementioned Alien Criminal Apprehension Program in 1988 (CAP, or Criminal Alien Program, since 2006). Inevitably, the prison population in the United States continued to grow (500% between 1980 and 1994), a trend intensified by the enactment of the Violent Crime Control and Law Enforcement Act of 1994 via its proposed enhancement, both in scope and in degree, of the provisions set forth by the Comprehensive Crime Control Act ten years earlier.[169]

Despite its intentions, the ACAP failed to deport a significant number of offenders. This was due to the fact that most drug-related offenses were perpetrated by individuals who had been residing in the country for a considerable amount of time, a status that deemed them as non-deportable, in accordance with provisions in the Immigration Reform and Control Act of 1986.[170] This shortcoming would

---

169. Macías-Rojas 60.
170. Statistically speaking, and not without a sense of irony, the longer a non-native born resides in the country, the more prone he/she is to break the

be addressed by the Illegal Immigration Reform and Immigrant Responsibility Act of 1996 (IIRIRA). As such, the Act included provisions designed to expand grounds for deportation by, on one hand, including minor offenses and, on the other, removing certain legal protections such as court hearing procedures for many deportation cases. It even implied that "green card holders convicted of even the most minor of crimes could be stripped of their legal status and shipped out of the country."[171] This erosion of individual and civil liberties was perpetuated under the guise of the legitimate pursuit of law and order and in the name of a national security agenda in the wake of the Oklahoma City bombing.

Consequently, INS detention beds almost doubled from 6,000 in 1995 to 11,500 in 1997. The number continued to rise as to reach 16,000 by 1998.[172] In an inevitable sequence of events, the expedited removal of individuals also increased, expeditiousness which likely included circumventing the courts and therefore trampling over due process. Low ranked immigration officers were substituting for judges in prescribing deportations as condoned by the IIRIRA.[173]

Indeed, immigration enforcement has become increasingly detached from the framework of the judicial system and the

law. Likewise, and contrarily to the perception suggested in much of the political discourse, crime rates among the native-born citizens are proportionally higher than those amidst the foreign-born population.

171. Walshe, Sadhbh. "'Operation Endgame' and the profitable purge of legal immigrants." The Guardian. Guardian News & Media Limited, 11 July 2012, theguardian.com/commentisfree/2012/jul/11/operation-endgame-purge-legal-immigrants (accessed May 15, 2018).

172. Macías-Rojas 63.

173. Even in those cases where non-citizens appear before a judge in immigration cases, they are not offered the option of obtaining the services of a court-appointed public defender, in contrast with what the law establishes for legal representation in other cases involving criminal proceedings— even though clandestine re-entry into the country is considered a criminal offense.

constitutional base on which it stands, thus widening the gap between the rights of the native born and those continuously eluding foreign citizens. In fact, once an immigrant's record is stained with a criminal offense, he/she is stripped of the right to a legal hearing before an immigration judge and may, instead, be placed on a fast-track removal process. In addition to the plea bargain route, the reinstatement of a previous removal order becomes likely, and the expedited removal looms larger in cases where the apprehension occurred within one hundred miles of the border or at a port of entry. Moreover, ICE agents may decide on someone's immediate deportability based on a previous aggravated felony conviction or even on some kinds of misdemeanors.

As recently as 2000, the INS exercised a certain degree of discretion regarding whom to arrest, interrogate, or deport, awarding special consideration to elders, children, and women, while also taking into account the length of residency in the United States and the criminal history of illegal migrants. The reaction to the events of September 11, 2001, however, significantly deprioritized these humanitarian concerns via the enhancement of mechanisms of detention, again at the expense of constitutionally protected freedoms and Supreme Court rulings alike, such as those regarding unlawful and indefinite detention in the absence of formal legal charges. While the dissolution of personal rights condoned and propelled by the Patriot Act was mostly aimed at Muslim and Arab individuals, the execution of its provisions collaterally affected the Hispanic population. Not only did it allow for measures dealing with "suspects of terrorism" to be artificially extended towards immigrants from the south, it eroded any leeway such individuals still enjoyed in what deportation and indefinite detention was concerned. This came not only by way of intolerance towards the unauthorized presence of "aliens," but also as a consequence of further swelling the immigration-related prison population. Between the detention of individuals perceived as posing security risks (most never charged with any terrorist activity) and of many merely for immigration violations, by 2001 INS's detention capacity had surged to 19,000 and eventually to 34,000 by 2012.[174] Furthermore, the justification for increased budget of the newly-created Department of Homeland Security was emboldened under the pretext of the "war on terrorism," but would inevitably put immigrants at large in a greater risk of incarceration and deportation. The fact that the agency's funding came now directly from the federal government altered the DHS's relation with local police forces along the border, as their priorities were impelled to change via financial incentives from law enforcement to immigration enforcement. This shift catalyzed the multiplication of detention facilities at the service of immigration enforcement, which naturally spurred detention rates and further added to the deportation tide. On the other hand, and because the Department of Homeland Security sought to prioritize the processing of immigrant criminal offenders and expedite their removal, as noted above, the persecution of criminal transgressions (rather than immigration-related ones) became the agency's focus, which invigorated the punitive paradigm associated with or under the pretense of immigration control. By transcending other considerations, longer-established foreign born individuals and even citizens increasingly became the targets of the incarceration and deportation frenzy. It becomes thus apparent that these procedural criteria foreshadowed more grievous ramifications, inasmuch as they seem to draw a line, arguably void of constitutional legitimacy, along ethnical lines as a mechanism of social control. Whether by contingency or by design, the current paradigm accentuates the schism between those who belong and those who do not. This logic of exclusion has long been a source of contention, and has

174. Macías-Rojas 74.

permeated the history of the country since the arrival of the first pilgrims. As David Bacon points out, racial bias was the bedrock on which legal status rested according to the first immigration laws of the country: "A Chinese worker who entered the country after 1882 without paper-son documents was illegal. An Italian who entered the same year at Ellis Island was not."[175]

But we need not go so far back to find more examples of this political arbitrariness. The American relationship with Cuban refugees acutely illustrates these rationalized decisions and laws.

According to the Cuban Adjustment Act (CAA) of 1966, permanent legal residence would be granted to any citizen of Cuba who had entered the United States after 1959 and who had been physically present in the country for at least two years. This was complemented with an equally generous policy of allowing permanence in the United States to all Cubans who were intercepted in U.S. territorial waters. During the Clinton administration, the application of the CAA was revised, and Cubans apprehended in escape vessels along the U.S. coast were no longer eligible for admission, but were rather sent back to Cuba or to a third country. However, the "Wet Foot, Dry Foot"[176] policy, as it became known, continued to warrant the lawful admission to those who managed to set foot on American shores. These Cubans would then enter expedited channels of legalization, which allowed them to apply, eventually and voluntarily, for U.S. citizenship. This policy remained in effect until 2017, when the

---

175. Bacon 206.

176. Or "wet feet, dry feet" policy, resulted from the 1995 revision of the Cuban Adjustment Act of 1966. The policy dictates that Cuban nationals intercepted in U.S. waters (wet foot) be returned to Cuba, while anyone of the same origin managing to reach shore ("dry foot") would be admitted into the United States and qualified for an expedited legal permanent residency application. Prior to 1995, reaching U.S. territorial waters was enough for any Cuban to be admitted legally into the United States.

Obama administration revoked it during its last days in office. But at the time of this writing, a Cuban citizen who presents him/herself at any port of entry along the U.S.-Mexico border is allowed to enter the country as a potential asylee and is granted the chance to apply for legal permanent residency on that basis.

Unfortunately, Mexicans and Central Americans do not benefit from the ideological obstinacy of the U.S. government in confronting the "autocratic bastion of communism" it deems Cuba, thus opening its golden gates to its "oppressed citizens." Haitians and Dominicans, to whom no policy even remotely resembling "Wet Foot, Dry Foot" was ever applied, were rejected as the Coast Guard invariably turned their vessels around back to their respective islands of origin. In practice, the law makes it illegal for some what is perfectly legal for others, voiding the much proclaimed assumption of equal opportunity and non-discrimination on the basis of national origin. As I suggested above, immigration law and policy seem to fall outside the realm of common law, as well as, arguably, that of the Constitution.

Part 3
Female diaspora: double vulnerability

Of the twelve million undocumented immigrants believed to reside in the United States, somewhere between 40% and 45% are women, an estimate not far from the little above 50% female share among immigrants at large, regardless of legal status.[177] Because of the surreptitious nature of the enterprise, and therefore the low profile sought by the undocumented immigrants during the journey across the border and later upon settling in the United States, these figures are based, somewhat paradoxically, on statistics regarding detention of immigrants en route. The number of detentions used as a statistical point of reference include those of Central Americans in transit through Mexico carried out by the authorities of that country: 95% of the detained originate in Guatemala, Honduras, and El Salvador.[178]

While the female share among immigrants shows significant demographic variations by country of origin, there are common denominators among the experiences of women immigrants originating from certain regions. Such is the case of basic motivations for their displacement and the arduousness of their clandestine land

---

177. Zhou, Min. "Contemporary Trends in Immigration to the United States: Gender, Labor-Market Incorporation, and Implications for Family Formation." Vol. 2, num. 2, 2003, 77-95 (Migraciones Internacionales Series).
178. Kuhner, Gretchen. "La Violencia Contra las Mujeres Migrantes en Tránsito por México." Revista de Derechos Humanos - Dfensor. June 2011, 19-25.

journey towards the United States on the part of Mexican and Central American women. It is also of particular importance to note certain shifts in trends regarding the composition of these female migratory fluxes, as well as to the nature of their motives and, moreover, the impact of their presence.

Traditionally, women made their way across the border into the United States accompanying their spousal partners, and their role was typically limited to that of emotional support. Even if travelling alone, these women more often than not travelled north with the purpose of reunifying with their companions, and were thus expected upon arrival to assume the same type of duties they performed back home, mostly in the form of domestic and maternal undertakings. In the last two or three decades, however, women have taken a more active stance in the workforce. Consequently, as their presence in the job market became more visible, they also began to tackle the perilous sojourn into the United States alone in greater numbers. Furthermore, given also the increased difficulty and expense associated with traversing border(s) illicitly, women tend now to establish deeper roots in the adoptive country and thus substantially prolong their stay beyond what was customary during times of a circular migratory model.[179] More tellingly, women are increasingly economically independent and find encouragement for immigrating in reasons not necessarily correlated to dependency or on reunification with a spouse or family. Escaping either domestic abuse, social repression, or the overall state of violence in which some communities are plunged (particularly in Mexico) are among the chief motivations for the increased presence of female migrants in the United States, both legal and undocumented. Cruelty against women in Lat-

---

179. Other contributing factors are, for example, relevant social, economic, and demographic developments in Mexico, such as the increased violence— even in smaller communities— and the decrease of maternity rates in that country.

in America is indeed rampant, according to statistics published by the Economic Commission for Latin America and the Caribbean, in which Central American countries rank particularly high in terms of physical and psychological violence alike.[180] As a consequence, femicide rates in the region are equally disturbing. The origins of such unfortunate state of affairs can certainly be traced to the patriarchal inclinings of Latin-based cultures, but its causes do not end there. The neoliberal undertones of the economic reforms carried out in the 1980s by governments in Central America— privatizations, elimination of tariffs on imports, preferential treatment of large corporations, dismantling of unionized movements, crippling of social programs— contributed to the concentration of wealth in the hands of very few and consequently to a dramatic increase in poverty among the less privileged citizenry. Furthermore, these inequalities triggered the above mentioned various forms of armed conflict in Nicaragua, El Salvador, Guatemala, and Honduras throughout the decade, which generated further misery amongst the population of these countries and consequently a steep surge in migration headed north. In these circumstances, violence against women is amplified, hand in hand with higher levels of unemployment, alcoholism, and the general state of frustration and despair vis-à-vis the deteriorating living conditions at the bottom of the social pyramid. As a result, most Central American women make the bold and difficult decision to leave behind their communities, and often their families, to seek a better life across borders independently, irrespective of marital status. According to the *Consejo Nacional de Población*, only 10% of the

---

180. "ECLAC— Economic Commission for Latin America and the Caribbean." ECLAC: At Least 2,795 Women Were Victims of Femicide in 23 Countries of Latin America and the Caribbean in 2017, ECLAC, 15 November 2018, cepal.org/en/pressreleases/eclac-least-2795-women-were-victims-femicide-23-countries-latin-america-and-caribbean (accessed March 21, 2019).

women who were repatriated by either Mexican or American immigration authorities between 2010 and 2012 declared family-related motivations for their attempt to relocate north, which validates the assertion that the overwhelming majority were migrating for employment or other personal reasons.[181]

According to the same organization, the percentage of married Mexicans residing in the United States is similar among both males and females— about 62% in 2012. Even more tellingly, 44% of the Mexican households in the U.S. are led by women,[182] which is almost twice the proportion of those established in Mexico.[183] These statistics, while pertaining to only one immigrant group, are indicative of a general trend among other nationalities as well, in light of the aforementioned numbers related to the motivational attributes ascribed to the Central American women in transit though Mexico.

This level of personal and professional affirmation on the part of these women does not, however, always imply a de facto self-determination, since female immigrants often embrace the triple charge of conjugality, motherhood, and employment. The latter of these is seldom seen as optional, but rather essential for the survival and well-being of the family, both in the adoptive country and back home, where it is common for family members staying behind at the origin to be dependent on the remittances sent by those residing abroad. Many of these women leave "their children behind with

181. Mexico. Secretaría de Gobernación. Consejo Nacional de Población. Mujeres Centroamericanas en Tránsito por México con Destino a Estados Unidos. Boletín de Migración Internacional. 2013. (Año I, Núm. 2, 4). CONAPO is a Mexican governmental agency devoted to the study of demographic trends and movement of both resident and transient population in Mexican territory.
182. Roughly 2.1 of the total 4.7 million households, per numbers of 2012.
183. Mexico. Secretaría de Gobernación. Consejo Nacional de Población. La Migración Femenina Mexicana a Estados Unidos. Tendencias Actuales. Boletín de Migración Internacional. 2013. (Año I, Núm. 1, 4-10).

grandmothers, with other female kin, with the children's fathers, and sometimes with paid caregivers."[184] They leave to improve the prospects of their offspring, often reaching that end by, ironically, taking care of children of others in a distant land. Due to their undocumented status and the aggravated exigencies imposed by clandestine border-crossing, this transnational motherhood entails the separation of children from their mothers for years, sometimes even decades.

The gender of the immigrant population in the United States has nevertheless received modest attention in studies over the years and has been approached mostly as a statistical triviality. However, the broader implications for both sending and receiving nations go well beyond gender roles, ranging from changes in the fabric of the labor market to significant shifts in family structure. For example, studies suggest that a larger influx of undocumented female immigrants into the United States was pivotal in freeing the native born women to the pursuit of more career-oriented lifestyles by filling in for their American counterparts as caretakers of their children. Accordingly, this phenomenon had repercussions not only on the families left behind in Central America and Mexico, but also on those who employed the enlarged supply of inexpensive childcare labor in the United States.

The particularly adverse set of circumstances and anxieties undocumented female border-crossers endure in their treacherous northbound itinerary has received little notice, but it certainly deserves attention and is of particular interest herein. It is also important to acknowledge that as difficult as the journey north is for Mexican women, the undertaking is substantially more treacherous for their

---

184. Hondagneu-Sotelo, Pierrette, and Ernestine Avila. "'I'm Here, But I'm There': The Meanings of Latina Transnational Motherhood." Gender & Society, vol. 11, no. 5, 1997, 549.

Central American counterparts. Not only do they have larger distances to cover, they also have fewer networking options on which to rely during their travels, such as family members along the way. As distant as these relatives may be, they are a good resource for shelter or even financial assistance that Mexican women are more likely to benefit from than foreign nationals traversing the country. Moreover, Central Americans face the added hardships associated with crossing multiple borders before finally reaching the one dividing Mexico and the United States. These women face the unfavorable odds of getting through roughly 2,000 miles of Mexican territory undetected and, even more unlikely, in safety. Although more culturally akin to the population of southern Mexico, Central Americans stand out as they venture farther north into the Mexican heartland.[185] In the Central Plateau, ironically a traditional point of origination of Mexican migrants, Central Americans illegally crossing are often targets of abuse and exploitation on the part of Mexican authorities and are maltreated by ordinary Mexicans or even by fellow migrants with whom they come in contact. The most poverty stricken migrants favor routes along the railroad tracks, seeking to climb on clandestine and dangerous rides on cargo trains headed to the northern border. Crossing Mexico in this manner often takes weeks, if not months, as migrants set out along different railway branches, constantly having to hop on and off different trains while these are in motion. This in itself carries considerable hazard: an accidental slip of the hand or a loss of footing frequently results in severed limbs or even death to the least fortunate or physically able. Once on the train, migrants are exposed to an additional array of perils, from falling off the cars upon dozing off or being deliberately pushed onto the tracks to other

---

185. Past the state of Mexico, the routes heading north branch out. Consequently, migration fluxes are not as concentrated, which allows better prospects of a less conspicuous transit through the rest of the country.

forms of assault carried out by gangs, all often producing equally fatal consequences. Against this precarious backdrop, the occasional checkpoints staged by immigration patrols along these trails are the least of the migrants' concerns.

While male migrants are not immune to the aforementioned perils, the dangers loom even larger to women en route, in addition to the somber prospects of illness, infection, and hunger. The adversities are all too real in an environment characterized by a dismal lack of hygiene and proper nutrition. While both sexes are vulnerable to these menaces against which they have little to no recourse except in the occasional safe house,[186] an even more sinister outlook await women migrants. Especially, but not only when travelling alone, women tend to be a preferential target to all kinds of violence and abuse, sexual in nature or otherwise, insofar as any male they encounter along the way may virtually be a perpetrator of the most hideous crimes against them. One of the most obvious threats is the profusion of gang activity operating both on the railway and in the immediacy of migrant safe houses where many migrants find temporary refuge and relief. Gang members are notorious for not only assaulting and robbing men and women alike, they often rape and abduct the latter, holding them either for ransom, for forced labor (including as sex slaves), or to sell them to prostitution networks

---

186. "CEM - Conferencia del Episcopado Mexicano." Estudio Sobre las Casas de Migrantes Católicas, CEM, 1 June 2017, cem.org.mx/Slider/58-ESTU-DIO-SOBRE-LAS-CASAS-DE-MIGRANTES-CAT%C3%93LICAS.html (accessed March 21, 2019). Although official governmental numbers are hard to come by, data points to more than 75 casas de migrantes currently in operation in Mexico, most of which run by the Catholic church or its affiliates and generally in close proximity to the railroad. These shelters provide different types of assistance to migrants (who are mostly Central American)— from food to medical care, to a shower, to a night's rest. There is a limit of time migrants may remain at these shelters, and the separation of males and females while on the premises is the norm.

operating in Mexico.[187] Frequently, this delinquency relies on the collusion with train conductors themselves who, willingly or under coercion, provide criminals with information that facilitate the execution of such vicious acts. In other instances, not only coyotes, but also conductors demand sexual favors from the women in exchange for allowing them to travel on the train tops or for warning them of an approaching immigration checkpoint. This common perverse transaction is often facilitated by their own male travel companions, who use women as bargaining chips to warrant their own safety. Minors and pregnant women are not spared the brutality.[188]

Further encroachment on their human rights and dignity is frequently committed by municipal, state, or federal agents who are easily disposed to abuse their position of authority vis-à-vis vulnerable migrant women. Similar inclinations are to be expected from private security guards at the service of the railroad company, as well as from immigration agents on the payroll of the Mexican *Instituto Nacional de Migración*.[189]

Women who travel by road avoid some of these contingencies, but not all. Those who cannot afford the more upscale bus services usually resort to relying on more informal forms of transportation in trucks or vans, whether to span the Mexican territory in its entirety or in segments. Naturally, the level of accreditation of the chosen mode of transportation is in direct proportion to the safety it offers. Instances have been reported when women migrants were lured into affordable and safe conduit via informal channels only to find out they had been duped into a stratagem set to assault and abduct them

187. Girardi, María Amalia, et al. Mujeres Transmigrantes. Org. by Oscar Arturo Castro Soto. Puebla: Universidad Iberoamericana, Centro de Estudios Sociales y Culturales Antonio de Montesinos, A. C., 2010, 75.
188. Montaner, Mariliana. Mujeres que Cruzan Fronteras. Mexico, D.F.: Secretaría de Relaciones Exteriores de México, 2006, 12.
189. Kuhner, "La Violencia," 21.

for purposes akin to those described above. If not forcibly, women are often otherwise compelled to trade sex for transportation, food, clothing, shelter, or to avoid even worse outcomes.[190]

Although all women are susceptible of becoming victims of one form of abuse or another, indigenous females tend to be preferential targets. This is due to a disturbing history of discrimination and exclusion against the descendants of the original Mesoamerican peoples, tracing back to colonial times. Sexual violence as a systemic form of control and male dominance is a rationale not to be easily dismissed in this context.

The most conservative figures point to anywhere between 60% to 70% of the women who take to crossing Mexico become victims of some sort of sexual violence in the process.[191] Many endure and often succumb to vile acts of outright torture. The level of violence and sexual exploitation of women has assumed such proportions that many who embark upon such treacherous journey expect sexual assault as a norm, rather than as an exception. For that reason, many Central American women opt to take preventive contraceptive measures via the administration of a Depo-Provera shot, which prevents ovulation for three months and therefore averts undesired pregnancies in case of rape. This method is sadly but tellingly known in Central America as the "anti-Mexico shot."[192] The physical and

---

190. Dávila, Genoveva Roldán and García, Nancy Pérez, ed. Construyendo un modelo de atención para mujeres migrantes víctimas de violencia sexual, en México. Mexico, D.F.: Incide Social, 2012, 48.

191. Montaner 39. Undisputed statistics are elusive, because one can only estimate the predictably high number of cases of sexual violence that go unreported— either because of the level of distrust towards Mexican authorities, continued intimidation by the perpetrators, or simply due to hindrances caused by the stigma of shame commonly associated with the nature of the crime.

192. Organización de los Estados Americanos. Comisión Interamericana de Derechos Humanos. Derechos humanos de los migrantes y otras personas en el contexto de la movilidad humana en México. Edited by the Relatoría sobre

psychological repercussions of sexual assault go beyond pregnancy, however. As a result of the extreme violence of the attacks, victims of rape often suffer from severe gynecological complications. Chief among these are difficulty in, or impossibility of, getting pregnant thereafter, vaginal and/or perineal traumatisms, torn muscles, and other serious lacerations that often develop into chronic back and pelvic pain and even derangement of the digestive system. Besides the obvious consequences of sexually transmitted diseases, but equally disruptive of a normal life, common psychological disorders affect both the cognitive and emotional levels; these may include self-blame and reclusion under social pressures that tend to re-victimize battered women.[193] This list, by no means exhaustive, portrays a reality exacerbated by the lack of post-factum access to appropriate medical care, either upon arrival in the United States (where healthcare costs are prohibitive) or back in the originating countries, where conditions for the treatment of these infirmities may be far from ideal. Sadly ironic, many of these women who are subjected to despicable acts of violence on their way north are attempting to escape domestic violence at home, which, according to the aforementioned reports by the Economic Commission for Latin America and the Caribbean, disproportionately besets the Central American region.

Once at the final border, where migrants often arrive materially and morally destitute, women are in many instances forced into sexual labor in one of the countless "massage" parlors, hostess bars, and brothels that unabashedly operate in towns on the south side along the Mexico-US border. They are compelled by either swindlers,

---

los Derechos de los Migrantes de la Comisión Interamericana de Derechos Humanos. ser. L/V/II, num. 48, 2013, 95.
193. Dávila 50.

procurers, partners, or by the sheer burden of the circumstances.[194] Whether coerced or voluntary, this is oftentimes the last recourse many women have to survive and hope to acquire the means necessary to finally cross over into the United States. Depending on the severity of the extortion and the level of turpitude of the enforcer, many women never make it across and continue being tormented beyond the three months that seems to be a common length of time many female migrants endure in such conditions. One can only speculate how many of the lamentable victims of the infamous wave of femicides in Ciudad Juárez were related to quandaries such as these, since many of the bodies found were never identified.[195]

Such gruesome acts of violence and savagery defy reason, but given the nature of the crimes and the circumstances in which they are committed, rarely do victims come forward and denounce their aggressors. On the other hand, the more extreme the cases of assault, the more hesitant surviving women generally feel about sharing their stories, either with authorities or with other entities. This reluctance contributes to concealing these atrocities under a shroud of quasi-secrecy that pushes their trials onto the realm of the fictitious in the minds of those who are unable to conceive, even in abstract, such barbarity.

---

194. Studies have found that the overwhelming majority of female sex workers in Mexican border towns is of Central American origin— over 90% (Girardi 34).

195. While the provenance and number of women killed in Ciudad Juárez is not consensual, the year of 1993 is commonly accepted as the starting point of the mass killings— which are now morbidly tallied in the thousands in that city alone. A substantial number of these showed signs of rape and/or torture prior, or leading to death (Staudt, Kathleen and Campbell, Howard. "The Other Side of the Ciudad Juárez Femicide Story." ReVista, David Rockefeller Center - Harvard University, (n/d), revista.drclas.harvard.edu/ book/other-side-ciudad-ju%C3%A1rez-femicide-story (accessed May 17, 2018).

Paradoxically, it is precisely the unimaginable nature of the suffering and the gruesome level of violence many migrants endure that may desensitize more fortunate human beings to the opprobrium experienced by so many, as the former choose the more comfortable position of disregarding these realities as mere improbability.

For these reasons, it seems plausible that insisting on the somber depiction of the gallery of horrors transfiguring many migrants into infrahuman (and thus strangely incorporeal) beings may not prove to be productive. Instead, the following testimonies give a voice to some of those people who faced the inevitability of crossing the U.S.-Mexico border surreptitiously. By focusing on the perils they encountered, on the odds they defied, and on what they left behind, I ultimately seek to unveil the human beings behind the numbers and bring to the foreground the role of both men and women in the evolving composition of the immigrant population seeking relocation in the United States.

Part 4
Testimonials

The following are the stories of a few men and women who know too well not only the state of affairs in the countries they left behind, but also the perils and hardships associated with crossing the U.S.-Mexico border in contravention of immigration law. Their testimonials are based on the transcription and translation of interviews conducted in Spanish between July and November of 2017. Most interviewees are old acquaintances and friends of the interviewer, which the latter took as an assurance of a relaxed openness that instills confidence on the reliability and accuracy of their accounts. To protect their anonymity, each one of these individuals is identified only by his/her initials, gender (m/f), and place or origin (country or, in the case of Mexico, state). They all currently reside, most still undocumented, in the southeast region of the United States.

The casual and sometimes jovial tone of the interviews stimulated the use of informal registers of language, granting the narrative colorful tonalities that are impossible, if desired, to translate. Still, an attempt is made at transcribing some of the slang used, particularly when it pertains to jargon associated with stealth border-crossing or otherwise revealing of the roots and past lives of these migrants. Questions are few and as non-intrusive to the flow of the narratives as possible, while the answers are not always reproduced verbatim due to the circumstances disclosed above.

The interviews are divided into four groups— desert, river, *línea*, and dreamer. More than contrasting access points, this distinction relates to the different methods of unauthorized entry. Nevertheless, in several accounts it becomes obvious that both river and desert are combined in the hybrid experience of many migrants, namely those forced to endure more remote areas along the Rio Grande. The dreamer featured, although her story does not pertain to illegal crossing per se, is nonetheless relevant considering the present political environment, which could degrade to illegality hundreds of thousands of young men and women currently under legal, albeit vulnerable, status.

The challenges of illegal border crossing are not limited to distresses associated with tight spaces and the constant threat of being discovered by the American immigration services, as expressed by some of the interviewees. That is the case of those migrants who have the added disadvantage of having to cross Mexico as illegal citizens in that country, too. Hundreds of thousands of Hondurans, Nicaraguans, Salvadorians, and Guatemalans, male and female, old and young, risk their lives in this treacherous journey— as many as half a million a year, according to the Migrant Policy Institute.[196] While reaching the border of Guatemala with Mexico seems relatively easy and uneventful, crossing this large and culturally distinct territory is no easy feat. As I alluded to before, riding atop cargo trains through Mexico is the only option for the poorest among the poor, who are unable to buy from smugglers a relatively safer itinerary by road. "*La Bestia*" is the name given to the massive trains that transport main-

196. Villegas, Rodrigo Dominguez. "Central American Migrants and 'La Bestia': The Route, Dangers, and Government Responses." Migration Policy Institute, MPI, 10 September 2014, migrationpolicy.org/article/central-american-migrants-and-%E2%80%9Cla-bestia%E2%80%9D-route-dangers-and-government-responses (accessed April 15, 2018).

ly industrial commodities across Mexico headed north, some even across the border into the United States. Central Americans typically board these trains in the Mexican southern states of Chiapas or Tabasco, a mere couple of hundred of kilometers from the Guatemalan border and endure the 1000-kilometer journey to central Mexico. Here the network bifurcates and different routes lead the cargo to distinct points of entry into the U.S. border. The discomfort of the ride and the inconvenience of having to change train lines along the way is the very least of their concerns. As mentioned previously, in addition to the risks inherent to frequently getting on and off the Beast (many migrants have lost their arms, legs, or lives altogether in this process), these poor souls also have to withstand the gangs of criminals who raid these trains along the way and who proceed to rob, torture, rape, and kidnap them. When it's not the gangs, it's the Mexican law enforcement officers, be that federal, state, municipal, or immigration agents who cross the line of their duties and do their part in beating and extorting these undocumented and defenseless passersby. Additionally, the private security agents hired by the rail freight add to the regrettable roll of abuse of authority that all too often spawns brutality and theft. For good reason *"La Bestia"* is also known as the "Train of Death." Although only one of the interviewed describes experiencing this challenge, many more do, and their suffering must be equitably acknowledged.

In any case, this is not the story of heroes or bandits. Nor does it focus on the portrayal of the most harrowing episodes— not because they are uncommon, but because they are filled with such gruesome details as to pass as fiction, and thus have the counterintuitive effect of perhaps unconsciously desensitizing and even anesthetizing us to a reality affecting so many human beings. The experiences shared by these migrants, who consider themselves lucky simply because they survived to tell their story, grant a voice to an anonymous mass of otherwise law-abiding individuals who had the audacity to set out to confront unfavorable odds as a desperate attempt to ameliorate living conditions they did not create. Frequently the lives they aim at improving are not primarily their own, but that of their family members. In fact, their kin are invariably of great cause for sorrow and concern to them, either when they leave them behind with very little hopes of seeing them again, or when they partake of the sacrifice— and the risks— of migrating illicitly.

The first question each of these interviewees heard was: "Tell me your story."

Desert

AV (m), Mexico City

I crossed the border with an uncle, a brother-in-law, and another friend of mine. This was 16 years ago; I was 21 or 22 years old.

We first headed towards Michoacán[197] by bus, which took about three hours. That's where we met the first coyotes, who would be in connection with others we would meet along the way. Each of us paid USD $1,500 for the service at the time.

We arrived at a house[198] where we waited three or four hours. In the meantime, other people were trickling in, until it was 25 of us in total. We all then got on a bus headed to Piedras Negras,[199] close to the border. Each person had to pay for his/her own food, and so we had some money on us (about 2,000 pesos). "Remember, you are not

---

197. Mexican state to the west of the Federal District, where Mexico City is located— in central Mexico.

198. The reference to these "houses" is recurrent throughout the interviews. As a hideout coyotes use to move migrants before their next stop, these are often called "stash houses." The moniker is more appropriate when the trafficking in question is of illegal narcotics, although the expression is suggestive of the large numbers of individuals sheltered in these hideouts at any given time and the poor living conditions resulting thereof.

199. Northeastern city in the state of Coahuila, across the border from Eagle Pass, Texas.

going to the U.S., you are going grape harvesting in Baja California," they would instruct us. This was the story we had to tell at check points held by the Mexican military on the Mexican side. At some of these checkpoints, the driver would just give the soldier some money and they would let us through without asking questions. In Piedras Negras, they took us to a hotel where they put us 4 per room. We sat and waited for a day and a half. In the morning of the second day, we were told that they (coyotes) would attempt to cross us that afternoon. By 6 p.m. they ordered us "Get ready, we are going to try and cross." They took us first to a house. There they advised us to each get a jug of water and leave behind whatever we no longer needed (like backpacks) since we were about to cross. Then we started walking. We walked about thirty minutes. We could see immigration vehicles in the distance, but we were told not to worry, because we were still in Mexican territory. We were walking towards the desert.

So, you were walking parallel to the border…

Exactly. We were headed towards somewhere immigration trucks would not reach. We continued walking until eventually there were sixty of us, because our group met with another group that had arrived the day before. The group that had just arrived (ours) was moved ahead first, while the first group was left behind to wait.

Did they tell you why?

I'll tell you in a minute.

Were these coyotes the same ones from your first leg of the trip, or were these different ones?

Different, we had just met these for the first time. They were four. Two stayed with the first group, the other two led us. And so, when it got completely dark, maybe around 10:00 p.m., we started trekking

into the desert. We walked about two hours. We were told to be vig-
ilant, and as soon as we caught sight of any signs of immigration
enforcement, we should lie low and hide in the bush the best we
could. Still, two hours into the desert we got caught by the *migra*.[200]
It turns out that we were used as decoy, as a distraction so that the
first group would cross while immigration officers were busy with
us. A helicopter arrived, along with a few trucks and vans, and several agents who themselves said... well, the one who arrested me
said: "Look, don't worry. I know this is hard. Try again tomorrow.
But now we are going to take you in." And so they took us to what
looked like a prison complex. They took our information and put us
in the same trucks where we were brought in, and they drive us back
towards the border to deport us. They leave us at a spot from which
we had to walk about 10 minutes to reach the Mexican side. This was
about 2:00 a.m. The coyotes arrived and took us back to the hotel in
Piedras Negras. "Now rest," we were told "We'll try again tomorrow."
In the afternoon of the next day, they took us back to the same place
as before. The group from the previous day was no longer, they had
already crossed. Instead, another group arrived, and we repeated everything from the day before, only now we stayed behind and took
advantage of the distraction caused by the new group being caught.
We walked about six hours in the bush, in the middle of the night, no
lights. There were some trees and a lot of prickly bushes,[201] which we
often failed to see and touched, or even fell on.

Who was part of this group? Children, women...?

200. Colloquial term used to designate immigration enforcement.
201. Most likely a reference to the Senegalia greggii tree, also referred to as
"catclaw mesquite," "tear blanket," "wait-a-minute tree," and "catclaw acacia"—
a small shrubby tree commonly found in arid areas of the Southwest United
States. All these monikers are well revealing of the nature of this desert tree,
notorious for its strong claw-like thorns.

In our group, I remember only two women and no kids. There was a really fat guy, and he was having a hard time. At times he could barely breathe, let alone walk. We thought we was going to die. Our feet, arms and legs were a mess because of the thorns of these bushes. We were also completely exhausted by then and could barely stand. The coyote told us he believed we were on the U.S. side of the border. At some point, we got to a road and we were told we were to cross in groups of five and hide in one of three large containers (the kind that big trucks haul) that sat of the other side, doors open.

Trailers of the kind where people have died before...[202]

Exactly, that kind. We all ran across the road five-by-five, got in these empty trailers, and rested. We must have stayed there an hour. We were about five minutes away from a house controlled by the coyotes. The coyote warned us about the area: "Here you are going to have to be really careful and watch out, not for immigration agents, but for the police patrols. Don't take off running, because they will catch you and then turn you in to immigration— and that's when you get into a whole lot of trouble." So we were told to walk slowly and calmly until you get into the house. It looked like an abandoned house. We got in. The smell in there... it was awful. People had urinated and defecated all over the place, and it stunk like nothing else. Still, we waited there.

How big was this house?

It was small, maybe three bedrooms. It had no electricity, and so we were in complete darkness in there, stepping on God knows what. It was disgusting. The coyote told us that vans would be arriving soon

---

202. I was referring to the suffocation to death of 19 migrants in a sweltering tractor-trailer found abandoned near Victoria, Texas in 2003. More recently, in 2017, 9 more deaths were connected to similar circumstances in San Antonio, Texas.

and driving us off, ten at a time. He asked for all our Mexican money since we no longer needed it on the American side. The vans then took us to another house, maybe thirty minutes away. This house was a little more decent, but about the same size— three bedrooms. And there was more than one hundred guys in there, I mean in each bedroom! The heat... imagine one hundred people in one room in the middle of summer. We couldn't lie down, we could barely sit on the floor. A bunch of us... the smell of sweat... What's worse, we were picked up from that location only on weekdays. Since we got there on a Friday, we had to stay there through the weekend, until Monday. The coyotes went out and bought food to last us three days. But the idiots put it all in the fridge without paying much attention to it, as they were playing cards or whatnot. When we decided to eat, there was hardly anything left. Food for three days lasted half a day, everybody was starving, and many of us didn't get to eat anything.

Had you eaten anything this whole time, until you got to this house?

Nothing, just water, I was starving, I had not eaten anything in almost two days. After that, the coyotes decided to ration the food. They bought a couple dozen eggs, a package of hot dogs, and a bunch of tortillas. They gave us one taco and a glass of water a day, that's it. The whole weekend, we ate one taco a day. On Monday morning, they told us we would leave that day. At 10:00 p.m., a van arrived for us. Trouble is, they packed thirty of us in one van. It was one those large vans, maybe twelve seats, but they had removed the seats and had us arranged like this [*gesturing sitting down, head crouched over bent knees*], against the back of the guy in front of us. Four rows of five guys each, crammed like that. This was really hard. Not only because the seating arrangement was uncomfortable, they were not driving on roads, but rather off road, dirt roads, middle of no-where— lots of bumps. One guy couldn't handle it, he cried so loud, he begged to be thrown into the bush and left there to die. In fact, we were all crying in pain and desperation. We simply could not move, lie down, stand up or anything like that. The guy who was crying loud, we had him lying like this [*gesturing arms in the air*] on top of the rest of us. The van had no air conditioning, and we were not given any water. What was worse, we were sitting right on top of the transmission,[203] we felt like we were sitting on fire. And don't you think this was a newer van— it was super old, very hard suspension, shaking and sputtering to no end. When we arrived in Phoenix, at dawn, we could not even stand— and so they just basically threw us on the side of the road. We lay there maybe thirty minutes, on the ground, unable to stand. In the morning, our first coyote contact (the one we had met back in Mexico) joined us. He took us to eat grilled chicken and everything, really nice. He settled with the other coyotes and told us "Now we are getting back in a van, but only six at a time." The next leg of the trip would take us from Phoenix to Atlanta. It was much better. It was just the coyote, me, my uncle, my brother-in-law, and three more guys in the back.

How long did that take?

About day and a half, it was really far. And the coyote gave us only one meal this whole time. Apparently, we had not paid him enough as to include any more food.

And the other people, the other 24?

Well, they stayed in Arizona, or had different arrangements. We had paid for a "package" that included getting us to Atlanta. I was out of money, and I even asked the coyote to lend me some. What happened was the guy who was supposed to hook us up with some

---

203. This probably included the rear differential and drive shaft, all giving off tremendous amounts of heat.

cash in Atlanta was not in Atlanta— he was in Charlotte. And so he drove me to Charlotte so he could get his money. While waiting for my contact, I stayed at the coyote's house, with his family, his wife, his kids. The next day my guy arrived, we paid the coyote, and he let me go.

Why Atlanta?

Because that's where a cousin of mine lived, he was my contact. From Atlanta we went to Myrtle Beach and started working in construction. I worked there for about three months until I came here.

Did you consider staying in Atlanta?

No, there are too many people there. It felt like Mexico, really.

From the day you left home in Mexico City until you got to Atlanta, how many days was that?

About ten days. In between waiting and traveling, ten days, surely. But this may vary a lot. My brother-in-law, for example, one time he went to Mexico and he was back in just three days. He left on Thursday and was back on Monday. But it's not always like that, it depends on the coyotes and on other things.

How long have you been in the United States now?

16, 17 years.

You have not been back to Mexico since…

No, I haven't. It has gotten more difficult and expensive to cross now. And the worst part is not even that, it's the *Zetas*.[204] Those guys are worse than the *migra*, they charge people in addition to what we

---

204. Los Zetas is a Mexican criminal syndicate, considered one of the most violent cartels in Mexico.

pay the coyotes. Even if you pay $5,000 dollars to a coyote, you may have to pay more to the *Zetas* if they find you.

When immigration deported you at the border, they just took you back to Piedras Negras…

Right. Me being from Mexico City, they would not bother sending me all the way back.

Among the other people in the detention facility, were there Central Americans, too?

No, just Mexicans. Because the idea back in Mexico was to claim we were headed to Baja California, and so our coyotes only dealt with Mexicans as not to raise suspicion. Central Americans have it even worse than us because the soldiers can tell they are not Mexican. And that's why some of them resent us— although I keep telling them we are mistreated by Mexican military and police officers, too. And take our money alike, which is all they want. And since Salvadorans, for example, have less money than us, they can't afford to bribe their way across— and the guards let them have it.

We all do it out of need, considering what's going on in our countries. Of course I miss my country, but now that I'm older and more mature, and now that I have a family, I have no problem staying here. I am also fortunate to now have my mom and my sisters here, too. I don't have a dad, as he passed when I was eight years old. So, the motivation to go back is more to visit now than really to move back.

What was the most difficult thing you had to endure crossing over?

Walking the desert. It was six hours that felt more like twenty. First because it was pitch black, and we would constantly fall in holes or onto bushes. Get this, the coyote himself broke his nose that night. I swear! Granted, the coyote was high on cocaine. They all were, to be able to handle the pressure and the pain. They would all get together and snort the powder. We would come across all sorts of fencing, including barbed wire we would have to crawl under, or get through the middle. And so the idiot was telling us how to get through one of those obstacles and when he turned around he hit a fencing post with his nose.

It was that dark...

And he was super high. He started yelling at us as if it were our fault. He then bandaged it somehow until we arrived at the road. But anyway, that was the hardest part, because you don't know what you're stepping on. And it was super-hot, too! The gallon we took didn't last very long, and so we were parched most of the way. They tell us "This won't take long," and we believe them, we don't know. But it takes hours on end, all of us on the verge of passing out. Sometimes we would come across some really huge trees, big enough we could fit under, because there were holes on the bottom, almost like caves. The coyotes would tell us to get inside. The stench... it stunk to high heaven, because many others before us had used it for relieving themselves. But the coyotes pushed us in, threatening that they would leave us behind, as so we had to cope with the stench. It was horrible. And the van ride... I swear, all those hours crouched up like that, unable to move... and the first house... it's hard just thinking about it... three days in that house, days of pure desperation. The coyotes wouldn't let us hardly move, always telling us to get down and shut up. One hundred of us, no air conditioning, no water, no food but once a day. Hot outside, even hotter inside, with all those people. And the bathroom... that was the worst sight I have ever seen in my life. Just getting near the door made you throw up. But no one complained. The coyotes constantly threatened us with throwing us out and leave us at the mercy of the cops or the *migra* if we did. Of course you would lose the money you paid them. There were so many moments... when we finally got off the van... the pain in my back and legs was just unbearable. The hunger and thirst… all I did was swallow my own saliva just to feel something going down my throat. When one gets here, we start forgetting these things. I mean, not forgetting, but I just don't think much about those hard times anymore.

Thank God my mom and sisters didn't have to go through this, as they came over with visas. You know, fake ones, but at least they didn't have to walk the desert. My mom has crossed twice that way, actually. And in those days, I went all the way to the border and picked them up on this side. It took me three days to get there and back. But it was cheaper than buying the package that included transportation to Atlanta. That was in those days, when it was not so risky. Today, you won't catch me anywhere near the border in Arizona or Texas.

PT (f), Guanajuato

I left home on April 5, 1999. It was three of us— a brother-in-law of mine, a friend, and myself. We left Morelia[205] and headed to the border at Nogales.[206] We paid the coyote USD $1,800 each. For three days, we waited at a house in Nogales, because they said there was a lot of surveillance those days. The conditions in this house were horrible— one small bathroom for thirteen of us in the whole group. We would sleep on the floor, all of us. Then they put us in two trucks and drove us to some small town, can't remember the name, and from there to a hotel near the border. Everyone else who was cross-ing stayed at this hotel, lots of people in this very ugly place. We were told we would leave the next day, but that the coyote would not be

---

205. Capital of the state of Michoacán, in central Mexico.
206. The city of Heroica Nogales is located in the northern state of Sonora, bordering Arizona. On the other side of the border lies Arizona's largest inter-national border town, incidentally also called Nogales.

coming with us. We got on a bus to go to yet another location, very close to Arizona. Nineteen of us left that morning, and four more joined us later. And so we began walking the desert.

Were there other women in the group?

There were just three of us women. We were given a jug with water, that's all. I was so hot… we walked all day, until sundown. We rested a bit around six of seven in the afternoon and continued walking into the night after dark. We couldn't see a thing after dark, and they didn't even let us have a lit cigarette. We feared falling into holes and being bitten by snakes. At one point, they told us we would have to go around an airport. We walked about two kilometers to go around the fence one way, and another two kilometers back, to continue our straight path through the desert. It was a small airstrip, maybe for governmental use, which didn't use to have a fence, but it does now. And so that added to the walking because it was impossible just to get across it. We walked in line around the airport, and the coyote would be at the back erasing our footprints on the desert sand. We walked all that night and all of the next day. We walked for two days in the heat of the desert. The water we had was super-hot, too. My husband had advised me to bring serum in my backpack, and I think that's what saved me. I would wet my lips in it, and that kept a little hydrated. We had no food, really— just a piece of bread and some ham, which got back in the heat. Of course we couldn't just go to a store and buy food, we were in the middle of the desert. After two days, we crawled under a metal fence, I assume this was a border fence. Near the fence was a road mainly used by the *migra*, and so we were told to get as far from the road as possible, into the bush. And so we met another group that immigration had caught before. And so they tried again. They divided us up among four trucks, but drive only one at a time. A *gringo*[207] then came and picked us up. He was driving a van and had a dog with him. The coyote sat with him up front, but the driver told him to send me to the front seat instead because his dog did not seem to like him very much. This was after sundown. He drove us three hours to a house where we could finally eat something more decent— they ordered pizza for us— and shower. The lady of the house told me I could stay with her, because everyone else were men. This was a decent home, clean. They then took the guys elsewhere, but I went to the house belonging to the coyote's sister, in Tucson, Arizona. The plan was for me to fly to the East Coast from there. She bought me new clothes and helped me put some makeup on, so I wouldn't raise any suspicions –but then we backed up because the *migra* had just caught two hundred migrants at the airport. I was there fifteen days, waiting for a day when there was not so much security checks at the airport. The day never arrived, and eventually someone from here had to go down to Arizona and get us. We were picked up at a gas station in a red convertible sports car, which was too small for six of us. We drove fifteen hours to Amarillo, Texas and from there we changed cars. Then we get pulled over, thankfully not by immigration, but by the anti-drug police. They asked us where we were going, searched the car, searched our bags, but didn't ask us for any ID. We didn't tell them we were headed to the East Coast, either— we told them we were close to our destination. They let us go, and we drove another twenty hours or so— straight, stopping only for gas. Thankfully I was never caught, and so they never fingerprinted me— unlike many of the people in the group, who had been caught several times.

---

207. Vernacular term designating a citizen of the United States, although not necessarily derogatory.

Why did you come?

I came for something better. My (ex)husband was already here, and the plan was to stay for two or three years and try to get ahead in life. But it ended up being nineteen years, and counting. We left two daughters behind with my mom in Mexico, nine and twelve years old at the time. I haven't seen one of them since. The other, the younger one, I didn't see for seven years, until she came and joined me here. I haven't seen anyone else in my family since then, except for my sister, whom I saw in Chicago for the first time in seventeen years.

Since leaving Celaya, how many days did it take you to arrive at your final destination here on the East Coast?

Twenty days.

Of all you had to go through, what part was the most difficult for you?

Leaving my family behind. More than walking the desert, the heat, the thirst, the hunger, the discomfort— was the feeling that I would not see them anytime soon.

But now you can, right? You divorced your husband and married an American citizen...

Well, not yet. Because I came in illegally, the lawyer says the process takes about ten years. And to get pardoned, I will have to move back to Mexico and live there five months, apparently. We'll see what happens.

RA (m), El Salvador

As Salvadorans, they call us *3-veces mojados*. [208] There was a lot of poverty back home, and so I decided to come. This was in 1998,

---

208. "Threefold wetbacks." Reference to the fact Salvadorans travelling by land

when I was seventeen. I came alone, with a coyote who was going to charge me USD $3,500 upon arrival in the United States. I traveled by bus from my village to the border with Guatemala, which took about twelve hours. And that's where my problems began, at the border with Guatemala. They asked me for a passport, but I didn't have one, or any other documents, for that matter. I mean, I did have a passport, but I left it home, as they recommend us not to carry anything that may make it easier to identify us as Salvadorans. Because if we get caught at the border with the US and deported, it's best to be sent back to Mexico, so it's easier to try another "jump" and not having to travel all the way from El Salvador again. I gave the border guards two hundred quetzals[209] and they let me through. Then it was another twenty hours by bus to cross Guatemala headed north, to the border with Chiapas.[210] The border with Mexico was easy to cross, we just crossed the river by boat. We were then picked up by a truck so old it could fall apart at any moment, the kind they use to transport cattle. Once we got to the city, in Chiapas, we traveled by bus. The only thing was that we had to stop every once in a while and pay 200 pesos to whomever stopped us— the Mexican military or the Federal Police— to get through. They would just come on the bus and start asking around for *papeles*,[211] but the only *papeles* they were interested in was the paper money kind. And so we pretended to be sleeping in our seats, but we would leave the 200 pesos visible and in reach. They walked by, got their money from each one of us, and leave. And

have to cross three international borders to reach United States' soil, therefore carrying the status of illegals across three different nations— Guatemala, Mexico, and the United States.

209. Guatemalan currency, valued at about 7-to-1 against the U.S. dollar at the time of this writing.

210. One of three Mexican states that border Guatemala. The others are Campeche and Tabasco.

211. "Papers," meaning documents.

we would be on our way again. The coyote had given me pesos beforehand because he knew how all of this would play out. So, the bus ride was tranquil. We did spend a lot of time in Villahermosa.[212] The coyote left us in a house there, about twenty of us, and he didn't show up for five days. There was no food, there was nothing. There was a mango tree in the back, which had unripe mangos on it. But it was all we had, and so we ate them all. After five days, I ventured out and went to a store nearby to buy food. When I came to the register to pay for what I had grabbed, a couple of guys approached me and robbed me. They beat me up and took all the money I had, so I was no longer able to buy anything. On day six, the coyote finally shows up— although drunk and high. So from there we continued by bus all the way to Matamoros, coughing up cash at every checkpoint along the way. When Mexicans got on the bus and saw us, all dirty and all, they would say "*ahí van los pollos*, there go the *pollos*."[213] Other than that, it was not too bad, except those five days at that house, where we almost starved to death. After that, my coyote claimed that my cousin didn't want to pay the amount they had agreed on to bring me, and so he was not going to cross me over. A girl who was coming with us, not because she needed, but to flee gang violence in Salvador, had a rich dad. Because I always watched out for her, she asked her dad to give me $500 dollars, and that's what convinced the coyote to bring me the rest of the way. I was stranded in Mexico City four months because of that, just going back and forth with the coyote.

Things got uglier when we crossed the border with the US. After a night in a dirty and stinky two-story house in Matamoros, about thirty of us swam across the Río Bravo[214] during the night. We put all our clothes in a plastic bag and held it in one hand, while trying

---

212. Capital and largest city of the state of Tabasco.
213. Colloquialism for "illegal immigrants" in Mexico.
214. Known in the United States as Rio Grande.

to swim with the other. We didn't want our clothes to get wet, it draws too much attention. Four pick-up trucks were expecting us on the other side, but not right on the shore, we walked for twelve hours until we got to them. One girl who was coming with us in the group was not feeling too well, we even thought she was going to die. All of us guys had to take turns carrying her because there was no turning back now. Soon after we got on the back of those pick-up trucks and drove off, the *migra* started following us, and so we all jumped off the trucks and ran all in different directions. It was each man for himself. I hid in the bush and then came back to the river banks. I was very young, and being alone like that, hearing coyotes nearby [*imitating howling sounds*] I was scared. Still I tried to sleep until morning. By seven in the morning, I start walking along a nearby road. Two miles in, as I was very thirsty I knocked on the door of a house I came across to ask for water. They pointed to a container on the ground where they dog drank from. That's all the water I had, and I drank it. When I got to a bus stop, a girl who was waiting there asked me where I was from. "I'm from here," I said. She didn't believe me. "You are not from here, look at you, all disgusting looking. You were with that group the *migra* caught last night and escaped, didn't you?" I tried to deny it, to no avail. Then she said that she was the wife of the coyote, and took me to their place, where I reconnected with the coyotes. From there, they moved us to a farm somewhere in Brownsville. We were there for eight days, sleeping outside, as there was no house or anything. We had food and water, but the nights were unbearable. There were lots of mosquitos, and bad ones. During the day, it was the heat that got the best of us. Eight days waiting. The only food they gave us was ground beef. Every day, ground meat. I got fed up with ground beef, but that's all we had. On the ninth day, immigration started chasing us with trucks and a helicopter. I wanted to cross the river back, but I felt too weak. I was too frail to run in the middle of the wind spawned by the helicopter, and so they caught me. They took me to the famous *corralón*.[215] When they asked me where I was from, of course I said I was from Mexico. And so they start quizzing me about what different things in Mexico are called, to which I knew all the answers. Until they asked me about the white ball and the black ball. No one had told me anything about that in Mexico, and I didn't know what they were talking about. It turns out that in Mexico that's how they decide who has to do military duty and who doesn't. If you get a white ball, military service is optional for you. If you get the black ball, it's mandatory, and you'll have to do it. Since I failed to respond to this one, they found out I was not Mexican, because every Mexican guy my age apparently knows this. The other guy they caught with me got too nervous and told them I was Salvadoran like him, and that made it worse for me to lie about it. They then put me in a cell, in isolation, for twelve hours, without food or drink, as punishment for lying to them.

How many days were you there?

Well, at first they thought I was underage, because I was so small and had gotten thinner for not eating well. But I had just turned eighteen, and when they figured it out, they took me from where they keep the youngsters to the main prison, where the adults were. When I got there, this Mexican guy starts making fun of me, telling me I should be at home being breastfed by my mother. When I tell him to

---

215. "Big Corral," unofficial designation for the detention center run by the Immigration and Naturalization Service located about 40 minutes from Brownsville, Texas— the Port Isabel Service Processing Center (Soble, Ronald L. "Big Corral–End of Line for Many Aliens : Immigration: The South Texas facility houses illegal border crossers, primarily from the 'Central American Triangle.'" Los Angeles Times, Los Angeles Times, 26 November 1990, latimes.com/archives/la-xpm-1990-11-26-mn-3979-story.html. Accessed February 26, 2019).

go to hell, he goes and gets his friends and to beat me up. They cut my hair, too, which I had long at the time. I was there for eight months.

How were the conditions there?

It was ok, except that they would wake us up at five in the morning every day— for showering and for breakfast. I got along with most people there, people coming and going all the time, and so it was not too bad.

A cousin of mine finally bailed me out— he paid USD $8,000 to get me out. I kept receiving court notices after that, but I began ignoring them after the first two times I show up the judge didn't. I started working there, in Texas, before I came here. It took me one full year since the day I left my hometown until I started working— four months stranded in Mexico City and another eight months in prison in Texas.

Has anyone else in your immediate family come to the United States?

I was the first one to make the move, but since I've been here, I've paid for two sisters and a brother to come and join me. My youngest brother doesn't want to come, though. He says that the trip is too hard, and in El Salvador, if he wants to eat a mango he can just grab one off a tree, while in the US you have to buy it [*laughter*]. We all send money to our parents back home to help them out. At the time I left, we were very poor— my dad had a piece of land, but nothing on it, really. Since the war,[216] gangs started appearing and going around to businesses demanding *renta*.[217] "*Renta*" means if you don't pay what they demand, they'll destroy your property or even kill

---

216. Civil war fought between a military-led government and left-wing opposition groups. The conflict lasted from 1980 to 1992.
217. Literally, "rent." Incidentally, depending on usage, renta may also be translated as "income" or "hire."

you, and so everyone who has a business or any sort of property pays up in exchange for some security. One day, I was walking home from school, in the middle of the day, wearing a pair of sneakers my cousin had sent me from here. They were pretty, not something you saw there every day. Two guys cut me off, and one of them holding a knife. I traded my new shoes for my life. That's what El Salvador is like today, probably even worse now than when I left.

Do you remember the war years?

I do. I remember one day, I remember it was the Day of the Dead, because we were eating something we only make that time of the year, *calabaza enmielada*.[218] It was around 7:00 p.m. when the guerrilla showed up and started shooting and killing people. We were at the table when all of a sudden bullets start coming through the walls because the walls in our house were just boards. We all ducked and got under whatever we could, as not to get shot. But I was eager to eat that pumpkin treat my mom had just made, and when I grabbed a piece and put it in my mouth, it burned me and I screamed. My poor mother thought I had gotten shot. But no, I had just burned my mouth with the candied pumpkin. But anyway, I had two uncles who were each one on a different side of the war. And they shot at one another, even though they were brothers.

Of all you went through, what was the hardest for you to endure?

I didn't have it that bad. The worse, really, was those days when we didn't have anything to eat, and the beating I took at the store

---

218. Calabaza enmielada con piloncillo is a treat traditionally prepared for the Day of the Dead in Mexico (November 2nd) and in some parts of Central America. It is prepared by boiling water with cinnamon sticks and unrefined brown sugar until it reaches a thick, honey-like consistency. Chunks of pumpkin are then simmered in the mixture to absorb its sweetness and flavor.

when I tried to get some food. I was lucky, many die in the desert trying to make it across. Fortunately I was always able to help other people, especially women— lots of women were in our group when I came. It must be hard to leave someone behind in the desert, because you know you'll be leaving them to a certain death.

I'm happy I'm able to help my parents now. We were really, really poor. Our house didn't even have electric power or plumbing. No one in the village did, except in the very center of it. We had to get water from a communal well about five or six miles away. That was one of the first jobs I had as a kid, hauling four large containers of water to the house in a wheelbarrow, five miles each way. And I had to be quick, because if I got there too late, the well would be out of water for the day. I would leave at midnight and came back at five in the morning with the water. I was around ten years old then. My dad was always harsher on me than on my brothers because I was a rebel. But I'm thankful today, because I enjoy working— not like many others who prefer wandering around and stealing. I like to work and make my own money. I even paid for my parents to get plumbing and electricity installed in their place. That's life, we do what we can.

River

JM (f), Veracruz.

I came to the United States with my two brothers in 2004. We tried a first time with a different coyote. The plan was to cross us through the *línea.*[219] I think this was in McAllen— I remember tasting the food and thinking it was not like the food in Mexico. Even Coke tasted strange to me. They put us in a van where the driver and another guy had papers, and we were in the back sleeping, or pretending to sleep. But they suspected we were illegals and told us to step off the car. They detained us, got our fingerprints, and kept us for two days. They waited until they had a bus full of us to send us all back across the border to Mexico.

How old were the three of you?

I was fifteen. My oldest brother was 29, and the youngest was thirteen. We came because our mother decided to bring us, since she was already here. She sent us the money to pay for the crossing. A few days after the first attempt, we headed to Reynosa[220] and

---

219. "The Line" refers to the queues that are formed in the immediacy of land ports of entry into the United States where border patrol or customs agents check the documentation presented to them by prospective crossers.
220. Reynosa is a border city in the state of Tamaulipas. Across the border lies

stayed with some uncles. We had to wait because my mom had to save money to pay the coyotes, and she had run out after the first attempt— crossing via the *línea* is expensive. One morning we were picked up by a truck that drove us to a house, and from there to an isolated area on the side of the road where we were told to step off and start walking. It has been a while and I don't recall exactly how many days we walked, but it was a few days of walking on the fields. When we finally reached the crossing point, we had to cross a river. On this side of the border, they finally gave us food and drink.

During all the days of walking, what did you bring with you in terms of food and drink?

We had a gallon of water each, that's all. They gave us some food at the house, but my brother forgot to bring the backpack with the food and so we didn't eat anything for days. There were a lot of people from Central America in the group, all men— I was the only girl there, and I was scared. No one would share any food with us. They kept saying "Don't worry, we're almost there," but the "almost" took forever. We could barely make it, we were starving and exhausted. As we got closer, people began discarding their leftovers, and so we picked up some food to eat— a tortilla, or whatever we could get. The guys guiding us across the river were bad people, they treated us badly. They were always yelling at us, telling us not to pull one another, and threatening to leave us right there in the middle of the river if we did. They put me and my youngest brother on an inner tube, while the men were not sitting on these things, but just grabbing them, and swimming a little. This was early in the morning. And so when we reached the shore, we walked a few more hours to reach a house, like in a ranch somewhere, before leaving for Houston. They gave us clothes there (ours were all wet

McAllen, Texas.

from crossing the river)— they had lots of clothes there, plenty of sizes and all. We left our wet clothing, surely for other who would arrive after us, and so on. There were a lot of people in this house, and I met another woman there. At night, I slept next to her, away from all the men. It was a big house, but there were lots of people, too. My little brother had a bad foot (he even had surgery back in Mexico) and he could take no more walking. He told us just to leave him there, he didn't care anymore. After the river we walked maybe two hours in the sand, and that was really tiring. My oldest brother could no longer carry our little brother. A friend of my oldest brother, from our village, and who crossed with us helped him carry our little brother, thank God. It was very hard, a lot of walking in the wilderness— there were snakes and who knows what else. We ran out of water, too. I remember there was some sort of river, or pond, not sure— there were cows nearby— and everybody headed towards it to drink that water, even though it was nasty. When it was my turn, the water was so murky and muddy I couldn't drink it. I wet my lips and kept on walking. My brother told me I had to suck it up and drink that water, or else I was not going to make it. I refused to drink that nasty water. It saddened me watching all these people drinking that water, dirty, salty, and all. This was still on the Mexico side. We had to get rid of my little brother's water because he couldn't carry his jug, and so we ran out of water fast— two gallons for the three of us. From the coyote's house where they had us, they called my aunt, who lived in Houston, to come and get us there. It took a long time for her to get there, this house must have been far from Houston, and Houston is a big city. We stayed with my aunt about four days, because our mother was still trying to get the money to pay for our trip to the East Coast. When my aunt received the money from my mom, she got us tickets on a *pesera*.[221] It took us two days, driving all night. We got here at night. We were dropped off at a gas station, where my mom came and got us.

Since leaving your village until arriving at your mother's house on the East Coast, how long did it take?

I remember we left around my brother's birthday, which is in the beginning of August, and when we got to Houston it must have been mid-September. By the time we arrived in the East Coast, I remember it was just a couple days before my birthday, which is September 24. So, it took us over a month, about month and a half, since we left home for the first time.

As a female, I imagine you were fearful of all that was going on. Was is important your older brother was with you, to protect you?

I was very scared, there were lots of men, too many. I even remember counting them, there were more than twelve in the group. My brother was always with me, and the coyote always tried to get us through first (we had to walk in line), along with my brothers and my brother's friend. And then the other men. Most were from Central America, because they spoke a different Spanish than us. Thank God none of them ever tried anything with me— in fact they barely spoke to us.

They probably wanted to conceal the fact that they were not Mexican. Some maybe didn't even speak Spanish at all...

Who knows, they kept quiet most of the time.

---

221. In Mexico, pesera is the colloquial designation of a passenger van or small bus transporting people on a fixed route. The term originates from the name of the Mexican currency, the peso, and refers to the original price of each such trip— one Mexican peso.

In this month and a half, what was the most difficult thing you had to endure?

Well, the most difficult for me… you see, I didn't want to come to this country, I came because my mother told me to. My brothers and I were raised by our grandparents, on my mother's side. But when my grandmother passed, we didn't have anyone to take care of us in Mexico. And so we had to come, although we didn't really know our mother that well, as she had been in the United States for a long time already. I told her I didn't want to come, and she told me to come and, if I didn't like it here, she would let me go back to Mexico. When I got here, it was hard living with her, we were practically strangers to one another— and of course I wanted to go back. But she wouldn't let me, she tricked me. The walking was hard, and sleeping out on the fields and desert was bad, thinking about the snakes and lizards— we walked four days, and slept outside as many nights just to get to the river. But in spite of all these hardships, the most difficult for me was really to leave my *abuelito*[222] behind. When my mom[223] died, my grandfather gave in to alcohol, and my mom's decision to bring us was sudden. I remember exactly the way he sat in his bedroom, begging me not to leave him. So, the crossing was hard, but leaving my *abuelo* behind and all alone in Mexico was even harder. After all these years we forget what we went through crossing the border, but leaving my grandfather is something never forgot, nor I ever will. I get really mad when I hear in the news, sometimes, how we are not wanted in this country or whatnot, I didn't even want to come! I was made to come, and it hurts me still how I left him all alone. I am still not at peace with that. About a year later or so, my grandfather died

---

222. Endearing term for "grandfather."
223. The interviewee meant "grandmother" here, but the lapsus linguae is well telling of the relationship she had with her diseased grandmother, whom she perhaps even addressed as "mom," as her de facto mother.

and we were not even able to see him or attend his funeral… I would love to go back one day… I still imagine them there, alive [*sobbing*], but I know if I ever go back, the house will be empty and they will be gone. I resent my mother for this, up to this day. Sometimes we get along, sometimes we don't. Back then I was a minor and didn't have a say, so I blame her for dragging me to this country against my will. I'm glad I was in Mexico when my grandmother passed, and I was able to be with her until the end. But when my grandfather died, I was not there [*sobbing*], and I am still not at peace with myself because of that. I will never forget that, it was the most difficult thing I had to do. Not being able to go to his funeral…. all because of coming to this country. Supposedly we come here for a better life, by I don't live any better than I did in Mexico. My mom sent us money from here and we never went without food or clothing or anything. I came to this country to suffer, really… here, we don't even have a home, we live in a rented trailer! My mother's husband works in construction, roofing. Here we came to realize what this country is really about. When you're in Mexico, you think people here roll in cash and money grows in trees— but it's not like that. Life here is much harder than in Mexico. We could finally see how my mother lived, her suffering, what she went through to send us money back to Mexico. But I had to resign myself with this, it is what it is, we need to get ahead and do the best we can. Thank God she managed to bring all of us, and all my brothers are here. It's five of us. My elder sister came before me, and another one of my brothers came as soon as my mom saved the money to get him across.

MV (f), Mexico City

The reason I came from DF[224] to the United States is common to many women: I separated from my son's father, and sometime later

224. "México, Distrito Federal" is the common designation for Mexico City

he began faltering on child support— which left me with little means to survive and to feed my son, considering the difficult economic situation for people like us and the lack of jobs in Mexico these days. My sister was already here, and she began encouraging me to come and join her. And so when my son finished kindergarten, I decided to come. It was hard. I crossed over the river, but before that I had to walk five or six hours with my son to get there.

How did the trip begin, from the time you were still in DF?

Well, we had hired someone we trusted to cross us through the *línea*, which made more sense especially because my son was only five at the time. We first headed to Ciudad Victoria[225] and then towards the border, near Corpus Christi. But unfortunately, they caught the guy who was going to get us across, and so we could no longer do that. We were in Ciudad Victoria about a week, waiting. We stayed at a hotel there. I had never been to a hotel before in my life, and this one did not look like a good place. I had sold everything I owned in order to pay for all this for me and my son. My family in Mexico suggested I come by myself and left my son with them, but I refused to do that. And so the solution was to cross the river instead. The guy who crossed us was good people. He told me he would be crossing six Brazilian women along with the two of us. I was worried because my son couldn't swim… I was not worried about myself, but my son…And so at the river, the guy told me: "You are going to stay here, I'm not going to get you across yet. I'm going and try to find some inner tubes or something like that to help cross your son, because these waters can be tricky." He brought us to where the river was the narrowest, but that's exactly where the currents were stronger. In the meantime, the Brazilians changed their mind and

among Mexican— who often abbreviate it to simply "DF."
225. City in the northern state of Tamaluipas.

he was just going to get me and my son across the border now. We were already so tired after the long walk, and my son started crying begging me not to let him go by himself. "I'm going to die, mom" he would say— just imagine such a little boy saying these things. I tried to comfort him during the hour or so we were there, waiting. But he kept saying "Mom, don't leave me," and the coyote asking me to quiet him down, because the police on the other side would hear him and arrest us all. He then told us we had to leave everything behind— no bags, no backpacks, nothing. He also told me I had to get naked, as to lessen the weight during the cross! No way was I going to cross naked, what would I do once on the other side? And I didn't. My son had with him a brown comfort blanket he never went without. And so we left everything behind but the blanket— which later, when it got wet, it weighted the same as twenty suitcases. I didn't trust them completely with my son, and I followed right be- hind them. They were right about the river being tricky there. I got caught in a current and I was being dragged down. I barely managed to hold on to a branch leaning over the water. The coyote said "When I turned around I could no longer see you, why did you risk it on your own?" But I would never leave my son in the hands of others I barely knew. Once on this side of the border, we climbed over a little hill thinking we were home free. But we ended up spending the next six hours or so trying to get through all the vegetation. The choice was between getting all scratched up by walking through the bush, or crawling under all that mess. It was impossible to get through. It was super-hot, and all I had with me, besides the blanket, was a jug of water— which ran out while were there. I felt like I was going to faint, and my son's voice was coarse from crying so much. We ended up in the same sport we were before five or six times, after each vain attempt to get us through all the bramble. "You have no idea where we are and where to go, do you?" I asked him. "I do, I swear I do," he claimed. But the truth is that we kept coming back to where we started. "This is going to be the last time," he said. And so he climbed up a tree to get a better view of the terrain, and finally decided on a route. We then got to a field with rows of some sort of cultivation. And that's when it starts to rain. It was not just some rain, it poured! "That's just what I needed," I remember thinking. My son could barely walk by now, and neither could I for that matter, and I carried his blanket, which kept getting heavier and heavier because of the rain. In desperation I told the coyote "You really don't have a clue. Just point me in the direction of the border patrol, I'm going to turn my-self in and get a ride with them back to the border." But he dissuaded me, assuring me we were almost there. He gave me his cell phone so that I didn't feel like he would take off and leave us there, stranded. With all that rain, dirt turned into mud, and our shoes got stuck in the mud. On top of it, my son wore orthopedic shoes for a condition he had, making things even worse. I could no longer carry both my son and his blanket, and asked him to help me with one of them, which he did. We finally got to a road— lots of trucks going by, I re-call— and he said a white van would come and get us. He asked me for his phone back, but I had lost it. I didn't even notice dropping it or anything, but the fact was that it was gone. I was carrying my son and his blanket, a cell phone was the last thing on my mind. "What are we going to do now? I had all my contacts there," he said. We did see the white van go by, back and forth, waiting to receive a signal from our coyote. The coyote waved at them from the distance, but they were not really looking, because they were expecting a phone call with a more precise location than just the general area where the picking up usually happened. They finally saw us, since it had stopped raining and visibility improved. We then took off running towards the van, which was hard to do in all that mud. We got in the van, and drove off. Right behind us was a big truck, and behind that truck, a border patrol car. I got so nervous I started crying, but nothing happened. I think it was also because I was exhausted and weak. The guy who picked us up in the van took us to his place, a trailer where he lived with his family. The guy who was going to drive us to Atlanta picked us up after a day and a half there. Our coyote was a good guy, though. At the end, he gave me a Jesus medallion (I still keep it, hanging on a wall at home), and told me "Here, for protection. You'll see, you'll do well. We went through a lot, but you'll be ok now." We stayed a week and a half with the gentleman who was to drive us to Atlanta. His name was Raúl (*was*, because he passed since), someone the coyote knew. He had no feet, and he had to do dialysis every day. And so he said "When I feel a little better, I will drive you to Atlanta, so your sister can pick you up there." And there we were, not knowing a word of English and with barely any clothes on our bodies. I was wearing just one shoe, because I had lost the other one somewhere. Raúl not only gave the coyote money to buy another cell phone, he took us shopping for clothing and shoes. He was a good man. When we got in the car, he warned me: "There will be a checkpoint, and they are going to stop us, and the agent is going to ask you questions. You just have to do keep calm and answer 'Yes, sir' and we won't have a problem." If we do get in trouble, please tell him you don't know me, I'm just giving you a ride." Sure enough, we were stopped at the checkpoint. The agent peeked inside the car, looking around at us, at my son sleeping, at Raúl's small dog, and at the wheelchair in the back of the van (his van was customized for his handicap). He then asked me a question I obviously did not understand. "Yes, sir," I replied. That's the only English I knew, because Raúl made me repeat those words dozens of times the time before so I wouldn't forget them. I think he let us go because we looked so "normal."

Anyway, the experience was difficult— these things we don't forget easily. Still today, after ten years, every time I get mad at my son I remind him of how hard it was to get here. The poor boy had nightmares every night, I think for about six months we would wake up in the middle of the night, crying and saying the same things he said back then during the crossing: "Don't leave me, I'm going to die…"

How long did it take you since the day you left home until you finally say your sister?

Three weeks. Three weeks during which my sister knew nothing about where we were or what was going on. That was also because we didn't get to Ciudad Victoria immediately, it took us a good three days to get there.

It was only after the fact when I realized the dangers we faced. Looking back, I can't believe I put my son through all of that. At the time you don't think about it because you underestimate the dangers we were to encounter. It was the first time I had ever left my home, alone, just me and my son. My dad, to this day, still thinks we came across via the *línea*, as I never had the courage to tell him what we went through. Also, our coyote did not make a living off of that activity, because he was an acquaintance of a family member of ours, and he actually offered to help us across— charging relatively little, maybe USD $1,500 at the time. This was possible back then because it was easier than it is today.

What was the hardest thing to endure in those three weeks?

The hardest thing, really, was to leave my family behind. During the three weeks, I have to admit we were fortunate, in spite of everything. Our coyote was a good guy and I never felt threatened by him in any way. On the contrary, he would encourage us in the most difficult moments. Then Raúl (may God have him)… he was so kind. After the week and a half, he didn't really want to drive us to Atlanta, he wanted to keep us there with him. I kept in touch with him long after we left, until his death, practically. We were fortunate, like I said. Many others are not so lucky.

CR (m), Guanajuato

I left Celaya[226] in July of 1997. I left because I needed to help my family. It was eight of us, and the economic situation was not the best. I was the oldest sibling, at sixteen. I had stopped studying to help my little brothers and sisters. I started working when I was fourteen. My dad... he liked to drink a lot, and so he didn't care about us. I decided to come because I had a cousin who got people across, he was a coyote. He told me that he would bring me and he wouldn't charge me anything. My mom didn't want me to come, because I was so young and I didn't have anyone here to help me out. I did have family here, but I really didn't have a relationship with them. My dad, sure, he wanted me to come and help the family out. And so we left Celaya, and bad luck had it that the bus we were travelling in rolled over half way to our destination, which was Piedras Negras. Luckily, none of the injuries were serious. I was asleep, and so I don't really know how it happened. We had to break the windows and get out. They called in another bus, but I got scared. It was the first time I had left my hometown, and began having doubts about the whole thing. I think other people felt the same. And so they called in two buses— one to take a group to Piedras Negras, the second to take the other group back home.

Were they all migrants, on the bus?

I imagine so. Why else would a bunch of guys head towards the border from Guanajuato? They all travelled with backpacks, and everything... so, yes, we were all in the same boat, so to speak. I told my

226. State of Guanajuato, in central Mexico.

cousin I was not going, and so I returned to Celaya, along with four other guys. Three months later he was back and asked me "Are you ready?" And so we headed towards the border again. This time we made it to Piedras Negras without incident. It was more than 1,000 kilometers. We did go through three checkpoints in Mexico, where the army looked for drug trafficking and such. Each time we had to get off and bribe the soldiers. My cousin already knew this, and warned me about it. And that's why we had some money on us ready for this purpose. These guys were above the law, and so we didn't even try to question this, or even thinking of refusing to give them money— they would have no problem in just shooting you and leaving you dead on the side of the road. By the time I got to Piedras Negras, I was broke. My cousin was the one who had to pay for my food. We stayed in Piedras Negras about eight days, waiting for the right time to cross the border. Money was running low, we even resorted to panhandling, at the end. It was bad. We went door to door asking for money to eat. Those days the Mexican army had the border areas well secured throughout the area, due to drug trafficking, and so we couldn't cross the river. When the army left, about a week later, that was our chance. We left the town in the afternoon and we walked all night to get to the river. We walked and walked through bush and fields in the middle of the night— it was so dark we couldn't even see where we were going. And so we kept falling and hitting things.

How many were you in the group that night?

It was about 25 of us. We finally got to the river. The water flow was heavy, which made crossing it dangerous. And at night, on top of that.

Did you have water on you? Was it hot?

Yes, we had jugs of water. This was July, and so it was very hot, even at night. And we had some canned food, like sausages and corn. And so we began crossing the river one by one— walking as far as we could, then swimming. The first one to cross was a guy who was coming with my cousin, like me. The current was so strong he ended up really far downstream. My cousin warned the rest of the group "If you are not sure about this, not a problem— we come back another time." But we had come this far, we didn't want to walk all the way back, and then return here again. He was especially concerned with me, since he felt responsible for me. And so we all crossed. We took all our clothes off and tied them in a large plastic bag each one of us had with that in mind. And that's how we crossed, naked.

After reaching the shore, we walked for another two hours, in the bush. Good thing my cousin knew the area well, all the paths and hiding posts. By midmorning we arrived at a certain spot in the middle of nowhere where he told us we had to wait until dark. And so we sat there all day, in the heat. That kind of terrain didn't have any trees, just small shrubs here and there, so we couldn't even find shade anywhere. We protected ourselves from the sun the best we could, by placing clothes between two bushes and lying underneath, for example. After dark, we began trekking again. We walked all night and half of the following day— until we arrived at a place where we had to wait for night time again. All this in the middle of the wild. It was close to a town I don't remember the name of, but my cousin went there alone and brought us water and some supplies. At dusk, my cousin instructed us to start walking again. I don't know how the two coyotes (my cousin and another guy) knew where we were going, as I couldn't see a thing, it was so dark. At some point he said, pointing in the distance "When we get to that hill, that's where we're going to catch the train." But the hill was so far away, and it never looked like it was getting any closer, in spite of all the walking!

How were everyone else doing? Were you all young guys? Any women, elders?

No, just men, and we were all young. And still, there was one guy who was not doing too well. He was not old, but a little older than us, and he was having it worse than us. We ended up walking two days and two nights, the last of which we didn't have anything to eat. When we finally made it to the hill, there were some mesquite trees, and so we all reached for the berries in the trees and ate them.

And water...?

Well, we walked through some farms that had cattle, and so we resorted to drinking from troughs the farmers had out for the animals— nasty water most of the time, but that's all we had and the heat was unbearable. We would clear aside the green stuff off the top and drink.

Since the train did not come by every day, we had to sit and wait for it. We waited one day and two nights, eating berries and drinking green water the cows hadn't finished. During this time I began questioning the purpose of all this. So many days and ordeals... I was beginning to give in to mental and physical exhaustion: "What am I doing here?" I asked myself. We couldn't see a house, or anything— just bush and a tremendous heat. I thought we were all going to die there.

Also, this was not a train stop or anything like that, this was in the middle of nowhere. It just happened to be a junction of different tracks, where the cargo trains slowed down a bit to switch tracks. We had to run and get on. There was a road nearby (by nearby here, I mean a couple hours walking, and cars there were few and far in between), and the guy who was in the most pain said "If the train does not come by tonight, I'm going to head toward the road and wait until someone takes me— immigration, police, or whatever. I cannot take any more of this." About eight of us headed towards that road, in despair. This was no one's fault, we didn't know what days the train ran, or what day it was, for that matter. They left in the morning, and by the afternoon I began regretting not having gone with them, instead of staying with my cousin and the others. All day and all night, no train. By two in the morning, the coyotes wake us briskly and order us to get up and get ready. We see a light in the distance, the train was finally coming. The train had these round tube-like structures between cars, and my cousin said "I'm going to put you inside one of those. I will be nearby. If you hear me calling you, you come out. Otherwise, stay put and be quiet. If they get you before me, then you yell out for me, and I'll come out." This was because the train would go through immigration checkpoints. And so I got into one of those things. It was completely dark inside, and all I could hear and feel was the motion of the train [*producing train noises*]. When we were getting closer to the checkpoint, my cousin stepped off the train and ran alongside it warning us "Heads up, we are getting to the checkpoint! All be quiet and still!" And so the train slowed down and went through a section of track with huge lights directed at it on both sides. I heard someone getting onto my car and hitting the metal with something. It scared me. I couldn't decide if I should come out or not. I could hear dogs barking all over the place, too. I was really scared. I think I heard two or three guys coming out of their hiding places, but I decided to wait for my cousin's voice and stayed put. When I sensed the train gaining speed, I peeked out to see what was going on. All was calm, but I couldn't see or hear anyone. The next time the train slowed down, we were close to San Antonio, Texas. And that's when I hear my cousin telling me to step off and jump. "Jump? Are you serious?" I asked. He said "Yes, there's another checkpoint ahead, you have to get off now." And so I jumped, and rolled down on the gravel. I remember then running for about forty minutes, on what it looked like a dry river bed. We ran until we got to a bridge, where a couple of trucks were expecting us. There they (my cousin's connections) drove us to Seguin, Texas, where my cousin had family. We stayed there a week with them. We finally could eat and drink something! And take a shower, the first in two weeks!

And the rest of the group?

We were still together, but fewer of us— fifteen or sixteen now. Almost all of them were headed here to the East Coast, but some were headed to Chicago and New York. Those went on their own from Seguin, by bus. The others remained with my cousin. Normally, he would go back to Mexico from here, but this trip was special because he felt responsible for me. He got us all pilled in a truck, a small pickup truck that had the bed covered, and drove us all the way from Texas like that. It was more than twenty hours, maybe 24 hours.

How many were you now?

It was nine of us. We all managed to fit, like sardines in a can. We didn't even stop to go to the bathroom— we would pee into empty bottles we had with us. In the few stops he made, at a fast-food place or something like that, we couldn't even walk! The first time I tried to step off I fell flat on the ground and couldn't get up. I didn't feel my feet! We arrived at dawn, maybe one or two in the morning. We knocked at the door of some family members, but they wouldn't take me in, because there was no space, they said. So, people whom I had never seen were the ones that ended up taking me in, some of my cousin's acquaintances. It's hurtful when family lets you down. And they found me work, too!

Since the day you left Celaya until you got here, how long did it take?

Three weeks. I told my cousin I would pay him when I managed to save some money, which I did after a while. I handed him $800 dollars, but he wouldn't take it. He said "Give me just $350 to give the other guy (the other coyote was his uncle) and we're all set."

What was the most difficult of all?

It was when we were waiting for the train, when we thought we were going to die. In the middle of nowhere, no food, no water, surrounded by tarantulas, scorpions, coyotes, snakes and who knows what else. We couldn't even sleep in peace, fearing being bitten by any of those animals who could come out of the darkness at any moment. We were not to turn on any lights, or else we could be caught. A couple of time we say helicopters flying by, and we ran from that place to lie low wherever we could, under a bush, in a snake whole or whatever, as long as it was out of sight. It was tough.

AR, (m) El Salvador

Crossing illegally is tough for everybody, but even more so for those of us from Central America. That's why we say we are *3-veces mojados!* When one comes over, we don't know anything, you have no idea what you will be against. The crossing gets harder each day, too. When I crossed, it was a little easier and cheaper. Nowadays, it's very difficult and much more dangerous. Right now, I have an 18-year-old sister who's tried to come here, to get away from all the crime in El Salvador. She was caught and arrested at the U.S. border two days ago. We'll see how we are going to solve the situation. She left home about two weeks ago... that's how it is. We all know this can happen, and sometimes it does. It happened to her.

Where did you come from?

I come from a small town, a village, really, about hours away from the capital, San Salvador. My dad worked in agriculture, but we were very poor. I was the oldest of nine siblings (four girls, five guys), and

I began realizing there was no future for me there. I decided to leave El Salvador when I was eighteen. This was in 1998. My brother[227] joined me here about two years later, when he turned eighteen as well. So, I headed towards the capital, and then from there north, towards Guatemala, by bus. We crossed that border walking, across a bridge over a river dividing the two countries. We walked about two or three miles, until we got to a cab that was waiting for us. It then took us to a house from which we would proceed by truck.

Did you have a coyote?

Yes, all the way from El Salvador. At the time, I paid USD $2,800. Today they're charging ten thousand!

How did you get the money back then?

I know this is hard to believe, but my dad had a friend here, one of those really good friends who not only lent us the money, but who took me in when I first got here. Still, my dad had to sell some animals from the farm, cow and things like that, for the down payment to the coyote. The rest we pay upon arrival at the final destination we agree upon. Luckily, I didn't go through a lot— unlike others. My brother, for example, had a really hard time crossing. He was arrested and deported back to El Salvador the first time around, and it took him two attempts to finally make it.

And so we get on a truck, a bunch of us stashed like fruit or vegetables. We were sitting down but crammed against one another, like bananas. After that trip, we couldn't walk, I couldn't even feel my legs. And that's how we crossed all of Guatemala and part of Mexico— on roads so bad the ride was unbearable. Crossing Mexico was harder than Guatemala, and not just because of the roads. The

---

227. Interviewee singled-out this particular brother because I know him personally as well, although I did not have the opportunity to interview him.

authorities in Mexico can tell we're not Mexican and take advantage of us. The truck was pulled over numerous times, and each time our guide would step down, pay them the *mordida*[228]— police, army, immigration, whatever— and we would be on our way again. They really discriminate against Central Americans, not as much the people, but rather the law enforcement agents. This happened about every fifteen or twenty miles. One time, we were on a bus near Monterrey[229] headed towards Matamoros,[230] wearing our best clothes as not to raise too much suspicion to law enforcement when they pulled us over and searched us, something funny happened. I was asleep and someone woke me up to step off the bus, but I didn't want to get caught. If I opened my mouth, they would know immediately I was not Mexican. Three or four of us got off the bus and had to pay up. That's how it is in Mexico— if you have money, you keep going, if not, you're finished.

I remember walking on a riverbed for about two hours or three hours. The water level was low, but this enough to get us very wet. All of this to avert Mexican immigration, as this was still in Mexican territory. I traveled with the same group pretty much all the way, but sometimes we would join other groups going in the same direction. In our inner group there were fifteen or twenty of us, all Salvadorans, including many women. One of the girls broke her ankle jumping over barbed wire. We were still in Mexico, and so she couldn't continue. Gladly, one of the guides stayed behind and took her back. By dawn, around two in the morning or so, they put us on a barge to cross what seemed to be a lake, a big lake. There were all kinds of people there, from Mexico, El Salvador, Honduras, Guatemala, you

---

228. Literally, a "bite," common designation for a small bribe.
229. Capital of the northeastern state of Nuevo León.
230. In the state of Tamaulipas, the city of Heroica Matamoros lies across the border from Brownsville, Texas.

name it. A truck was waiting for us on shore, to take us to a house—this all on the American side now. We stayed there three days, a bunch of us sleeping in the same room, on the floor. Thankfully they fed us there. In the meantime, the guides were checking things out and see when the best time for leaving would be. They then took us by cab, three at a time, to another house, close to Houston now.

How did you cross the checkpoints?

I think I had a good coyote and a lot of luck. He must have had good connections, because he knew exactly what the best times were for getting across, when the passage would be clear— either because they were taking a break at the checkpoint or because someone working the checkpoint at a certain time was looking the other way, if you know what I mean. And this could be at any time of the day or night. And so we bounced from house to house in this manner.

How long did it take you since the day you left your village?

About a month. 28 days to get to the U.S. border, and then a couple more days go get out of the border region. From Houston, a van brought a bunch of us, about ten or twelve of us, and started dropping us off along the way to the East Coast. This was the most relaxed part of the trip— a seat just for me, no fear of being pulled over and shot. Like I said, I consider myself lucky, other people have had it much worse than me, and many don't even make it at all. My brother was in jail for a month, and they sent him back all the way to Salvador. After that he tried again. You see, the deal with the coyote included three attempts. If you get caught and sent back twice, the coyote still has the responsibility of trying to cross you one last time. After that, you lose your money, the money you put down, either half or whatever it has been agreed on. At the second attempt, he made it. Another brother of mine was caught, too. He told me immigration put him in a *hielera*,[231] as they call it. Two days, he was there. If you happen to be sick and end up in one of these, you will surely die there. They say it's super-cold in there, although I don't have personal experience. These people have no heart, they treat you like a dog when you don't have papers and even take pleasure in punishing us, migrants.

---

231. "Icebox" or "freezer," a reference to the extremely low temperatures in the cells used by U.S. Customs and Border Protection to keep its detainees, referenced above.

"La Línea"

JR (f), Mexico City.

I was 25 when I came to the US, about eleven years ago. I came with my two daughters— four and five years old at the time— and my mother. I didn't really want to come, even though everyone says there are more opportunities for you and for your kids. I had a good life in Mexico, although there is a lot of corruption and crime, which seems to be a bit more under control here in the United States. The main thing is that I had problems with the father of my daughters. In reality I fled my life in Mexico to avoid a possible abduction of my daughters or myself. I really had little choice, even though I had a good, stable, well-paid job. I was typical middle class, but I had to put the safety of my daughters first and come here. Since I had family here, they encouraged me to come, stressing to me that the girls would have better opportunities here. And so I started to get rid of everything you own, the few valuables that we owned. Once you leave, you don't know if or when you'll come back [*sobbing*]. The first difficult thing is really that, shedding away your life and saying goodbye to those you love— the family you leave behind whom you don't know when you are ever going to see again. And so we started selling stuff and began planning everything. We contacted some-one who had helped several people across the border, and therefore someone we could more or less trust. But we can never fully trust anyone. It was the first I ever left the country, and I didn't know what to expect. My biggest fear was because I had never taken such a long trip. We first had to get to... I don't recall... I think it was in Arizona. I really don't remember where exactly we had to get to, somewhere where there was a *línea*, near the border. Neither I nor my mom had the slightest idea of how to get there.

So, four of you were travelling...

Yes, my mom and I and my daughters. But we had no idea. We didn't know what route, what bus line, nothing. They told us to travel as light as possible, and so we didn't bring much with us. It was our family here that guided us every step of the way. First we were on a long flight, about five hours, then from there we traveled by bus, during the night if I recall correctly. When we arrived at the terminal, I remember looking around and all I could see was immigrants. Many people sleeping on the floor of that bus station— women, children, elders, all types of people. I even got a little scared, I confess. All seats were taken by immigrants, there was hardly room to move. We knew all these people were going to get across, we just didn't know how they would go about it. My mom and I looked at one another wondering if we were to stay here, too. The person who was taking us, however, told us we were getting on a cab and head to a hotel where we were expected. As soon as you step foot out of the terminal, people begin approaching you offering their services to help you cross the border. It was hard to elude all these people, these coyotes. All this was new for us, we had never seen anything like it.

What exactly was your plan?

We had a planned route to follow. We had no papers, of course, but we had a contact waiting for us there, and we just had to follow the instructions as to how to get to them. I still don't understand well what all those people were doing there at the station or what they were waiting for. I figure they came without a pre-defined plan, and so they may have been trying to improvise their crossing. We were fortunate that at least we had someone waiting for us, someone with a plan. All we were told was "When you get to the hotel, lock yourselves in. Do not leave the room under any circumstances, and do not answer the door to anyone. Don't even come close and peek through the windows." That's what we were told. It was almost like going to jail. That made us feel even more unsafe, since we had no idea why we had to be hiding like that. They also told us not to use the phone in the room— we would be in touch with them using only our cell phones. And so when we got to the hotel, it was scary. It was a very bad looking place. And so we got in our room and looked ourselves in, as instructed. But we could tell there were a lot of people in that hotel as well, I mean, people who would be crossing the border, people like us. We were told not to worry, and we hoped the next day everything would be a thing of the past. But we were left in the dark, so to speak, about what the plan was. "Await my call," that's all they told us. So, a day went by, we were getting hungry, but at the same time we had been told not to leave the room, that we could get robbed, or worse. I didn't know what to do, and I was most worried about the little girls. But we were not to starve, and so we left and started looking for food. Another day went by, and the feeling of un-certainty grew. No one called us, no one told us anything, we didn't know what to do. Until the day they called and said that the first ones to cross would be the girls. I was floored. How could I separate from my daughters? They explained this was the best and safest way, be-cause they would take them with other kids, a large group of school children who were legitimately crossing the border. I was not happy at all. We've heard so many horror stories of cases where parents lose their children forever. Or if they see them again, something really bad had happened— they were abused, molested, God knows what. All these ideas were crossing my mind as I begin fearing the worse. They were so little, and I didn't even know who would be taking them across. I was afraid they would hurt them, rape them, or force them to work as slaves. During this time all I did was cry, even though the people here kept assuring me they would be safe. I cried all day, I didn't want to let them go without me. The next day, they came to get them. I said goodbye to them, and the poor girls were scared too. "Where are we going, mommy?" they cried. I remember asking the older one to take care of her younger sister. I told them we would be together again soon. Even though I was trying to assure them, they asked me why I was crying. There was a woman in the group, and she told me not to worry. And so they took them away [whimper]. I was devastated. As soon as they left and we shut the door behind them, I fell on the floor weeping. And that's what I did all day in the room, always thinking the worse. I did not hear anything from them until about seven hours later. I wondered why it had taken so long, the border was right there. I was told "Your daughters are here already." I asked to speak with them, but they claimed they were sleeping and didn't let me to. How could I even sleep not knowing where my girls were and whom they were with? I didn't not get to talk with them until the next day. Even though were told they were safe and well, it was a bad day for me. I kept thinking they had fallen prey of men… you know, we always think the worse, after all the stories we hear and the kind of place we were in. It was the hardest thing of all— leaving your daughters in the hands of strangers. If something happened to them, I would never forgive myself for it.

How much longer did you wait in the hotel?

From there, my mom and I waited for… well, after being able to talk to my daughters, I felt a little better. I asked them repeatedly what they had eaten and if anyone had touched them, etc. They told me they were ok, and that the lady in charge of them was buying clothes for them, and that everything was going according to plan. That same lady told me on the phone to be calm, or else the crossing would prove even more difficult. Hearing from them really calmed me down, although the opportunities to do so would be rare. We would try and call these people, but they would never answer. They would only talk on the phone at their discretion, which was not much, and I could only talk to my girls very briefly each time. They told me that so much talking would agitate them, which would hurt the cause. I acquiesced, but we were still uncertain regarding our own fate. Entire days would go by and we wouldn't hear from them at all. We tried to call them all the time to find out what was going on, to no avail. Two more days went by and we didn't hear a thing from them. By the third day, we get a call: "We need you to come out and walk around amidst other people," they told us. We wondered what for, but all they said was "Come down to the lobby and head towards the avenue across from the place. We're going to take pictures of you." And that's what we did. At some point, a car with two women seating on the front goes by, and I hear a shout "Hey, you, turn around!" And that's when I see a camera taking pictures of me and my mom. The worse about all this is how we are given so little information and everything is so vague, so surreal. And so they drove off and we wouldn't hear back from them again until the next day. When they called, they told me they had arranged for an ID card for me, but they were still working on finding one for my mom. I assumed they were looking for people whose features resembled ours, so we could borrow their documents. Two days later, they brought us some information regarding names, addresses, etc. we were to memorize. Those would be our new identities, and they would match the information on the ID cards we were to use to cross. Later we were told to head out towards a certain kiosk nearby, dressed and with makeup on in such and such manner, as if we were going to such and such place. We were still getting ready when they told us to hurry and come down, it was time. We couldn't take anything with us but a purse, and so we left behind in the room everything else, the little we had brought with us. We were also told not to bring anything in the purse that would identify us, as we could be subject to search. We came down, and they gave us ID cards.

ID card? Not a passport…

No, just an ID card.

With a picture of someone who looked like you…

Yes, supposedly, although I didn't find any similarities, to tell you the truth. So much so I had my doubts this would work. The photo on my mom's card looked like her, but not mine, not at all. The person's face in the photo was too full, much darker than me, it was not even close to looking like me. Anyway, they gave us instruction on what to expect and what to do and not to do while crossing the checkpoint— the questions we would be asked, how to walk, where to look, what to say, etc. And so we walked towards a bridge everyone was crossing.

This was in Nogales…

It was. We were instructed on exactly what to do: the person going with us would go first, then, a few people later, one of us would go through (I had to say goodbye to my mom, in case one of us didn't make it across). Something happened, though— and I was told to turn around and come back.

Over the phone?

No, the guy who was crossing with us, one of the coyotes. You see, one of the coyotes goes through first, and we are to cross a few minutes later, accompanied by another of the coyotes who gives you instructions along the way, pretending to be talking on the phone but in reality telling you not to turn, to look up, etc. As I was about to reach the handrail (there were two, one on each side) he told be "Go back, turn around and go back." I was confused, but I complied. "I'm getting across, but you need to go back," he said. And so I started walking back towards an ice cream store nearby, as if I had forgotten something. "Don't look back, don't do anything to call attention to yourself," he said before we separated. My mom didn't even get onto the bridge, as she was behind me. We were then told that the first coyote who crossed informed the others that the agents were checking IDs too attentively, and thus the situation was not favorable. We waited for a call all day yesterday, to no avail. We knew they could call at any moment, and we had to be ready to leave. By 7:00 p.m. we figured we would spend at least another night in the hotel. I hadn't talked to my daughters in a long time and I was longing to see them. The day after we got the call, around 10:00 a.m. This time mom went ahead first. I could see she had crossed, but I was reminded not to make any comments, turn, smile, or show any reaction whatsoever. Then it was my turn to cross— no questions asked or anything, I couldn't believe it. The coyote behind be then said "You made it across." At the end of the bridge on this side of the border, we get to a pavilion from where they got us in a van. This was not over yet, as I then learned there would be checkpoints on the roads. We were disposed in a certain way in the van (they placed mom and I in the front), and we were told to look at the agents in the eye. We didn't even know if these would be immigration agents or the police. And so when we were stopped, the agent peeked in and looked around at all of us as we held our ID cards. They didn't make us step down, except for a guy in the back who was pretending to be asleep. It turns out he was with the group, acting as decoy.

They never told us of the possibility of us being asked to step off the car and be searched— maybe not so scare us, I think. We rode in this van for about half hour, until we got to a small bus station. They got us tickets and got us on a bus, assuring us we would be safe from scrutiny past that point. And from there we traveled about two hours, just the two of us. Another person then picked us up and drove us another couple of hours. It turns out this was the leader of the whole operation.

How did he recognize you?

Well, while in the van, they communicate via cell phone and co-ordinate everything. I remember them asking and confirmed our identities, as well as the estimated time of our arrival, etc. Out of seven in the van, only four were illegal crossers, and so we were easy to identify. When we got off the bus, he knew exactly who we were, even though the bus station was packed. He approached us and asked "Are you and you so and so?", and that's it. That's when he introduced himself, asked if we were hungry, if we needed anything. We hadn't eaten all day, but food was the last thing on my mind, all I wanted was to see my daughters. We arrived at this house very late, at dawn, I remember it was very cold. When I finally saw my girls, sleeping in a big bed, I couldn't help myself and hugged them, feeling relieved. The next day, our family members came to pick us up and it was all very exciting. We didn't even have breakfast, we couldn't wait to get as far from the border as possible. We made it all the way to the East coast in one straight shot, stopping only for gas and to alternate drivers among the family members who came and got us.

And so, how long did this whole ordeal take?

Between ten and twelve days since we left Mexico City. The drive from Arizona alone was almost three days. But really, the most difficult was the feeling of helplessness, of not knowing what was going on and whether I would see my children again. It was really exasperating. We were on the brink of despair, as the hours seemed like days, and each day, an eternity.

Thank you for telling me your story.

Thank you for listening to our stories. I know there are many people who have it much worse than we did, others who never make it. And many who don't see their children again. The first thing I asked my daughters when I finally had the chance of talking to them alone was "Did they touch you? What did they do? Who bathed you?" One of the girls had a bruise, and I asked her how she got it. She told me she fell in the tub. I wanted to ask them all the details and make sure they had not been molested or anything like that, but thankfully they said the lady was the only one who took care of them. It's difficult for me to talk about this to this day.

RR (f), Mexico City

My husband and my brothers were already in the United States, and so after a while my husband encouraged me to come as well. I told him wouldn't venture the trip by myself and that he would have to come and get me. And so my husband, even though he does not have papers, went back to Mexico to bring us.

How long had he been in the United States already?

About two or three years. And so we flew from Mexico City to Chihuahua,[232] I believe it was, I don't remember right. Maybe it was Sonora.[233] I know it was close to the border. From there, a cousin of mine recommended we contacted a person who helped her cross. At

---

232. The largest of the Mexican states, it borders the Southwest of the United States at New Mexico and Texas.

233. State to the west, bordering mostly Arizona.

the hotel, they told us not to use the landline in the room, because the lines were bugged. And that other coyotes rob people. They said to my husband via cell phone, that they would come by and talk that very evening and decide on what to do. The coyote told us they would cross the boy first, our 6-year-old son.

How old were you then?

Around 27. And so when he told us he would cross the child first, I got scared. I didn't want to let our son go with someone we didn't really know, right? Although he was well referenced, we were skeptical. He told us we had no other choice, really, and we accepted. The man came back the next day just so we, and especially my son, would familiarize ourselves with him. In the meantime, as we walked around a mall, he instructed the boy on what to say— that his name was so and so, that he was his uncle, what his new name would be, etc. And so the next day they came for him. A few hours later, they called us telling us not to worry, our son was safe and sound on the other side of the border. Now we would have to about crossing ourselves. The original idea was to walk across, by because my husband was in poor health, we had to think of something else. We were there two weeks, separated from our son, although we spoke with him on the phone often. After the first week, they told us they had found a *mica*[234] for me, but not for my husband, and that's what the holdup was. Another week later, they came back with both ID cards and a lot of instructions: we had to memorize our new identities, addresses, etc. If we were asked, we

---

234. Mica is slang for "Border Crossing Cards" (and sometimes to other types of laminated ID cards), the kind mentioned before by another interviewee, for entering the United States from Mexico. The U.S. embassy used to issue this type of document to frequent border crossers, which has since been replaced by the standard visa inserted into passports.

were to say we had come to work on the strawberry *pizca*.[235] That day the people that got us across were not the same that crossed our son, though. They sent some kids, sixteen or seventeen years old, to do the job. I couldn't believe it. They gave us the last instructions on where to go and how to act— and that they would be in touch in case we were caught to discuss a way to get us out. We paid the money…

How much did you pay?

For my son was 12,000, and 25,000 (Mexican Pesos) for each one of us, my husband and me. I remember well, because we saved for a long time for this. We gave them a part before the crossing, and the rest after the crossing. They cut my hair and put makeup on me to make me look like the person in the picture ID. Although she did look like me, I was still scared. I had no idea what I was going to find there. They said: "Look, we are going to coach you"— and they proceeded to tell me exactly how to position my body, how to look at the border agent, how to answer the questions, etc. Then they quizzed me on my new identity and on all the information I needed to use in my answers, in case I was to be asked. Same with my husband. They also took away all my original documents— driver's license, voting card, all of that gone, as not to expose my real identity. They told us the people getting across with us had legal papers, and that a car would be expecting us on the American side. Looking back now, I really don't know how we pulled it off. I remember my hands shaking! But I went ahead, followed all the instructions— I looked at the agent right in the eye, and after five or six seconds, not having been asked any questions, I went ahead and went through, hands shaking and all.

---

235. Colloquialism for "harvest," from the Nahuátl "pixca"— meaning "collecting," "gathering," or "harvesting."

And your husband?

We went through at the same time, just in different lines— I think there were three lines in total. My husband took a little longer, and all I could think of was his ID card and how bad it looked. I though he was going to get caught. But no, a few minutes after me, I saw my husband coming through. They did intercept one of our guides, because he appeared with hair on this card, but now he was bald. But because his papers were legit, we just had to wait a little longer. After thirty minutes or so he came out and we were ready to leave. And that's when we finally could see our son, at the house they drove us to. He was so happy to see us and us to see him! But we were not out of the woods yet, since we still had to make it to my cousin's in Colorado— and therefore make it through possible checkpoints on the way. We were to drive two cars. The coyote would go first and see if there were any checkpoints, and in case there were, he would signal with the brake lights three times, after which we would turn around and go back to the house. Thankfully, there was no checkpoint, although we did see the spot where the checkpoint normally is. My husband was driving, and he was worried because he could barely see the coyote's car far ahead, as it would be suspicious to drive too close together. We caught up with him by a little store, when he told us we were home free. And that's it— we rented a car in Colorado and drove all the way to the East Coast. That was our experience.

How long did it take you since you left your home in Mexico until you arrived at your final destination?

Almost a month, if I recall correctly. At least three weeks— two weeks alone were spent waiting on the other side of the border. From stories I have heard, I admit our experience was easy— others have it a lot harder, and many never make it at all. My brother, for example, and my cousins, they crossed the desert, one of them was even pregnant at the time. And they told me about the fear they felt, running and crawling through the bush while hearing the border patrol dogs behind them. Compared to them, I had it easy. I didn't even come across a checkpoint, nor do I know what the *migra* looks like! We were blessed.

"Dreamer"

MM, (f) Durango

My parents and I came to the United States from Durango[236] in January of 2007. I was twelve. My parents owned a little business, but the violence in Mexico was getting to a point they feared for our safety. For example, there were groups coming by the business and demanding money in exchange for "safety"... so, we came with a tourist visa, which was valid for six months. We stayed longer than that, of course. My aunt was living here already, and so we came here directly. When we first got here as a child, I knew I was undocumented, but I didn't really know what that meant in practice. Until I went to high school, when my friends and classmates began obtaining their driving permits and applying for colleges— and I couldn't. It was very difficult for me to accept that. From an early age I dreamed with going to college, but then realizing I was not going to be able to do it hurt. It demotivated me. My parents told me not to worry, that they would find a way for me to continue studying. I was taking honors courses in high school, I was playing soccer, and I was a member of several student organizations, including those related to community service. During my third year in high school

---

236. State in northwest Mexico whose capital is known by the same toponym, shortened from Victoria de Durango.

I realized undocumented students were not eligible for financial aid or scholarships. What's worse, we had to pay out-of-state tuition, too. I was really upset. One of my teachers recommended I looked into private schools, maybe because they were not associated with the State, they would not hinder me so much. And so I did— got accepted into the two schools I applied to in the state. I graduated from high school in June, 2012, with a 4.0 GPA, top 1% in my class. That same month, President Obama established the DACA policy, to which I applied— although I still completed my first year at one of the private schools that accepted me. After the first year, I began working that summer— because now I could. DACA allowed me a social security number, a work permit, and protection against deportation— all valid for two years, after which I had to apply for renewal. I then transferred to a community college, taking three classes while I worked full-time. I studied there two semesters, and that's when I transferred to a public school. I still had to pay out-of-state tuition, though— and continued being ineligible for financial aid. I got some scholarships that helped a lot. This is my third year at this school, and I'm graduating in May. It was good being able to work and going to school legally, as well as being able to drive without the fear of being caught and deported. The problem is that I am studying to be an elementary school teacher, but DACA does not allow me to pursue any professional teaching licenses. As it stands, I will not be able to become a teacher because of that. It's sad, because I've taken and passed Praxis I and Praxis II,[237] but it's not going to do any good. It may get worse if the Trump administration decides to discontinue the DACA program. I've worked so hard to get to where I am, and seeing all taken away like that [*sobbing*]... it's very hard. Because even though I wouldn't be able to teach in this state, I was willing to

---

237. Praxis tests are a series of teacher certification exams administered by the ETS, or Educational Testing Service.

move to another one where that would be possible to get a license— but not if DACA gets taken away. My permit expires in 2019, and if Congress doesn't come up with a solution, I won't be able to work in the profession I chose [*sobbing*]. I have been rethinking my future, because everything is now uncertain. I don't know what's going to happen or what I will have to do. Much of the Hispanic community was hopeful for a Hillary Clinton victory, but when reality dawned on us, it was a rude awakening. All in my family (and beyond) are now afraid of what's to come next— raids, arrests, deportations, etc. I can only imagine so many other students who have not yet started college, or just started recently, I can only imagine the fear and uncertainty. If they are not allowed to renew their status, they won't be able to finish and graduate. I myself was planning on doing study abroad my last year, but that became impossible now.

Do you know many students like you, DACA recipients your age?

I do. I have a friend who's in Medical School at Loyola, in Chicago. She's in her second year, and she fears she won't be able to finish her degree. I have another friend who graduated two years ago in Biology and Spanish and who was planning on applying to graduate school. Not sure she can do that now. Another two friends of mine are graduating in December. All DACA students. Many DACA recipients are building their lives around it— not only studying, but also working, getting married, buying cars, buying homes, forming families— trying to live a normal life.

How do your parents feel about this?

They are worried. But they have gone through so much, though, this is really not a surprise. They are more worried about me than about themselves. We have nothing for us back in Mexico anymore, and so going back is really not an option. We built our lives here. I grew up here, I really know no other homeland. In the meantime, violence and poverty have not gotten any better in Mexico. Most my family, except a grandmother and a couple of aunts, are here and in California.

Do you have any alternative plans?

Well, if I am not allowed to teach at a school in the state... I did some research and found an organization called Teach For America, which apparently works with DACA recipients who want to teach and find places where they can be teachers. That was my plan to circumvent the fact this state won't allow me to obtain a professional license. But if they end DACA altogether, I will be living back in the shadows again. They told me they are still accepting applications, but my contract would be at the discretion of the school district— which means they could revoke it as soon as DACA is phased out. I do not have any other option at this point. I hope Congress does what's right, I mean, how are you going to throw 700,000 people into illegality just like that? How are you going to take away something you gave them— mostly hope?

Conclusion

The sizable presence of undocumented immigrants in the United States, as well as the continual trickle of new migrants that persist in entering the country illegally at great risk to themselves and often their loved ones, was not created in a vacuum. Rather, it is the result of a complex conjunction of forces both at origin and destination. As elsewhere in the world, the pressures at the root of the displacement of large swaths of population from their home regions and countries are the systemic agency of political and economic designs emanating precisely from those receiving nations such as the United States of America. In *They Take Our Jobs!*, Aviva Chomsky gathers a few examples that summarize how by its very nature, colonialism (and, by inference, neocolonialism and imperialism) produces migration, thus leading to an inevitable juncture where "the empire came home," as Eliot Dickinson so deftly puts it.[238] In *Blowback*, Chalmers Johnson summarizes this process well when he bluntly decries that "refugee flows across our southern border" tend to originate in "countries where U.S.-supported repression has created genocidal conditions or where U.S.-supported economic policies have led to unbearable misery."[239] Furthermore, these economic policies are dictated for no other reason than the "preservation of property relations and other

238. Dickinson 53.
239. Johnson, Chalmers. Blowback. New York: Metropolitan Books, 2000, 17.

institutions on which rest the interests of our own wealthy and priv-ileged minority"— in the words of whistleblower and former CIA agent Philip Agee.[240]

This phenomenon is not unique to the United States, since "dis-placement has been indispensable to the growth of capitalism from the beginning," as David Bacon observes.[241] In fact, the globalized market system as it began taking shape in the 1500s, with its "inter-national division of labor and an unequal exchange of goods that reinforced the economic development of core countries and under-development of peripheral countries," has been at the center of mar-ket-driven economic doctrines since the dawn of mercantilism.[242] This formulation has only been accentuated by the rapid process of deindustrialization of those core countries' economies, along with the corresponding shift to their financialization that began tak-ing shape in the 1970s with the United States at the wheel of such trends. The application of global free-market economic policies in resource-rich but otherwise poor nations exploit the citizenry in the lower rungs of society, who are then impelled to migrate, either to larger urban areas within their own countries or abroad. This has certainly been the scenario in Central America (and in other Lat-in-American countries farther south) where the neoliberal dogma was imposed with great violence throughout the 1980s and enforced with iron fist against the best interests of the populace.[243] These poli-cies generated massive displacement in the region and provided the backdrop for the surge of migration fluxes originating in Central America after said period. Regrettably, the global capitalist complex

240. Agee, Philip. Inside the Company: CIA Diary. Bantam Books, 1975, 617.
241. Bacon 68.
242. Dickinson 53.
243. Kelly, Lara. "Neoliberalism in Latin America." Citizens' Press, CP, (n/d), cpress.org/editorials/old/neoliberalism-in-latin-america (accessed May 8, 2018).

is deeply committed to the free movement of capital and goods across all borders, but not that of people — who turn into *illegal* while fighting for their survival since the system does not assent to legal immigration in any meaningful way, in spite of deep-seated assumptions to the contrary.

But despite vociferous calls for strengthened border control and the barrage of arguments, usually and paradoxically from the Right, to curtail immigration, the fact is that those who have clout over political decisions are not actually in favor of such actions, simply because the maintenance of a status quo of abundant labor, low wages, and a compliant workforce depends on a generous and continuous flow of migrant workers, preferably illegal. The role of the corporate community in acting as a regulator to such flow has been particularly blatant in the case of Mexican migrants ever since the U.S. economy became dependent on cheap labor for its vigorous development in the 1800s. This contradiction is the reason why immigration policy has historically almost exclusively focused on border control and only residually on labor interests that keep providing the demand for a submissive workforce. Ironically, it is exactly tighter border controls that have made remigration more difficult and hampered the circularity of migration (especially Mexican), as undocumented foreign workers began opting to remain in the U.S. for fears of difficulties in reentering the country. In the meantime, any enforcement campaigns carried out at places of employment invariably place the burden of proof on employees— not on the employers, who can always claim good faith in their hiring practices. Whether by design or not, the looming threat of deportation produced by the INS serves best, in practice, the goals of the latter, insofar as the fear it instills in the former curbs any attempts at unionizing undocumented workers may feel inclined to pursue. Accordingly, the inability to protest and organize thus contribute decisively to keeping wages low, safety regulations out of scrutiny, and workers' rights overlooked. More-over, this intimidation, rather than encouraging migrant workers to leave the country, further socially isolates them, forcing them to live in the shadows and naturally dissuading them from fully integrating into U.S. culture and society.

On that note, it is precisely those tactics, coupled with a funda-mentally broken immigration system, that play squarely into the na-tivist anxieties regarding Spanish-speaking immigrants' reluctance to "assimilate" into American culture (or its Anglo-Saxon features presumably). This construct is mainly predicated on the use of Span-ish and thus revealing of a populist aversion to and rejection of mul-tilingualism and multiculturalism.[244]

The fear of the unassimilated "other" is perhaps best epitomized by the $263 billion that has been spend on border and immigration enforcement since 1986.[245] An even more important figure is that of the number of mortal victims— 10,000 between 1994 and 2018[246]— who succumbed, and continue to succumb, to the hazards such dan-gerous undertaking presents. It is unfortunate how these numbers seem to correlate.

There is indeed a crisis at the border, but it does not display the sordid contours relayed by ideologues whose agenda is promoting a fear-mongering perception whereby herds of criminals and even

---

244. Tirman, John. Immigration and the American Backlash. Cambridge, MA: MIT Press, 2015, 147.

245. Schwartz, Mattathias. "'Come On Down to the Rio Grande Valley. I'll Show You Around.' Would patrolling with the Border Patrol change your mind about the border?" New York, New York Media LLC., 6 January 2019, nymag. com/intelligencer/2019/01/border-patrol-texas-immigration.html (accessed February 24, 2019).

246. Ryon, Sean. "Aid, and agua, along the border." Nation Swell, NationSwell, 11 July 2018, nationswell.com/water-station-mexico-border (accessed Decem-ber 15, 2018).

terrorists are invading the country via the southern border. Rather, the real crisis is ascribed to the deplorable living conditions that so many of resorting to crossing the border surreptitiously endure at home; to their exposure to unimaginable hardships associated with the journey; to the physical and psychological distress caused by the endeavor, even if successful; to the human loss represented by those who do not succeed, and end up trading lack of positive prospects at home for death abroad, to the millions who are doomed to live on the margins of society, as second-class citizens. There is no doubt as to the seriousness of this humanitarian crisis.

Solutions to the problem can only be found by first acknowledging and addressing its root causes. For such, it will take political good will and vision, perhaps to an unprecedented extent. As a first step, it is crucial to repudiate the rather abstract notion of what an *illegal immigrant* is and to acknowledge these human beings' exceptional sacrifice and honor the dignity they merit. After all, "life, liberty and the pursuit of happiness" are "unalienable rights" accorded "all men," who are, moreover, "created equal"— meaning regardless of nationality or citizenship status.

Afterword

Diniz Borges
Director of the Portuguese Beyond Borders Institute
California State University, Fresno

The American story is a story of immigrants, past and present. Our unique mosaic is a fusion of many identifies, religions, cultures and languages, unified in a basic principle, and best described by Robert Kennedy when he wrote: "Our attitude towards immigration reflects our faith in the American ideal. We have always believed it possible for men and women who start at the bottom to rise as far as the talent and energy allow. Neither race nor place of birth should affect their chances." If America forgets this basic premise, then America is stepping away from its true uniqueness, from its noble mission of being more than a place or a nation, but really an idea and a beacon of hope.

It is a country of many paradoxes, the America that my maternal grandfather emigrated to in 1910 and left in 1928. The country that my parents emigrated in 1968, bringing me and my 3-year-old brother, has been both a land of opportunity and land of discrimination. Our collective history as a country of immigrants hasn't always been the most consistent. Indeed, it has remained a rollercoaster of policies and legislation that opens and closes many doors, as

Pedro Lopes masterfully indicates in this well studied and poetically written book. The historical context given by Lopes, along with his well-researched chapters on all the various components of the different epochs and measures that have made up the migration from Latin America to the United States, affords the reader the opportunity to go beyond the vague headlines, the manipulated narrative for dogmatic gains and the simplified media soundbites, that entice emotions on both sides of the partisan spectrum and leave us with a hollow and deranged collective outlook on such an important part of the American cloth.

Immigration is indeed a complex topic. The current political climate, albeit amplified to the point that elected public entities won't even look at trying to resolve pertinent and urgent issues, hasn't happened in a vacuum. *Crossing Borders* is clear and unequivocal in laying out the historical context that permeated the contemporary situation. We arrived at our present impasse in immigration policy due to a conjunction of past policies and practices. Pedro Lopes eloquently creates the chronological lineage that carried us to today's world. A moment, and let's hope it is indeed just a moment, that allowed the nation, in an disturbing and disgraceful way to turn our back on Emma Lazarus' words: "Give me your tired, your poor, Your huddled masses yearning to breathe free, The wretched refuse of your teeming shore. Send these, the homeless, tempest-tossed, to me: I lift my lamp beside the golden door."

The human stories featured in this book, through the engaging interviews, brings us in direct contact with men and women, whose hopes and aspirations, dilemmas and challenges, and above all whose sense of determination is in a realm that middle class America may have forgotten, or placed at the bottom of our communal memory box. Reading these first-hand accounts, and living through their words the unthinkable situations that many had to endure to come into the United States, makes me, as an immigrant, a proud immigrant, feel that I was privileged. These unsung heroes, with their fortitude, their sacrifices and their unwavering commitment to have a new life in the United States, are enlightening and inspiring. They are real American stories. As psychologist and author Mary Pipher wrote: "They bring us gifts. We can synthesize the best of our traditions with the best of theirs. We can teach and learn from each other to produce a better America." The stories of these modern-day fighters for the American idealism, currently vilified through yet another wave of nativism and political expediency, are part of who we are, for as President John Kennedy said: "Everywhere immigrants have enriched and strengthened the fabric of American life."

Crossing Borders gave me yet another perspective on immigration to the United States. Its historical context and its first-person interviews, along with Pedro Lopes' captivating prose remind me that although the trajectory to America is never easy, the journey of those who come from the various Latin American countries has been, and continues to be, beyond arduous. The conditions that these men, women, and children endure are unthinkable. Their willingness to give all they have, even their lives, in order to have the crumbs of American prosperity and build a better world for their children, even if only within the periphery of our society, is truly inspirational. More than moving, these stories, along with our history, must be the impetus we need as a society to move forward, to call out the injustices, to question the racial inequalities and the racism in our current immigration policies, to stand up for human rights for all, to go beyond the malicious terms we give those who by their actions and their grit, coming from far-a-way places, perhaps, are the true believers in what we like to coin as: the American Spirit.

Acknowledgements

Expressing gratitude can be an act of probity as much as an exercise of deceit, often simultaneously. On one hand, and for fairness sake, we must abandon the pretense any human accomplishment (or mere survival, for that matter) can ever be attributed to the agency of a sole individual, and thus coming to honor those who were there along the way is an observance of the most basic of principles. On the other hand, this symbolical salute inevitably and invariably falls short of acknowledging all who were influential, to *any* degree or capacity, in *both* assisting in the completion of this type of undertaking *and* in the forming of the individual who puts his/her name on the cover— or else this portion of any book would be longer than all the rest.

Aware of such limitations, a special word of appreciation to all of my friends who kindly agreed to take some time out of their busy schedules to share their stories with me, and whom I'll acknowledge only by their initials: A.V., R.A., J.M.G., M.V., J.R., R.A.R., C.R., P.T., A.R., and M.M.; along with many others who, although not interviewed for this work, contributed decisively to my instruction on the subject I bring to the fore herein. Of these, a special mention to my dear friends José Páramo (now enjoying legal status in the U.S., upon marrying an American citizen) and Guillermo Álvarez (who has since returned to his natal Mexico). They were also my first teachers of Spanish, by the way, a fact which not only made the interviews possible, it had changed my life, quite literally, by the time the first words of this project were typed.

I am also profoundly indebted to my wife, for her constant encouragement and support; to my dear colleague Dr. Carlos Mentley, who to continual reassurance, added several semesters of favorable class scheduling which ultimately allowed me to dedicate undivided attention to this project; to my office neighbor, Dr. Sean Barnette, who continues to serve as my personal grammar consultant; and to my dear friend Dr. Amy England, who kindly accepted to revise the manuscript.

Stepping further back, a tribute to my parents, who always had formal education in exceedingly high regard and always urged me to pursue it— this in spite of not having had the privilege of benefiting many years of studies themselves, for modern standards. Instrumental to that end were all the educators in front of every classroom I ever sat in, as latterly as my last college professor and as remotely as the school teacher of whom I have my earliest memory, D. Maria do Carmo.

By the same token, and as a critical complement to academic experience, I acknowledge the role of all the authors I ever read and all the ideas to which I have otherwise been exposed, for whereas it takes a village to raise a child, it takes a much larger community of efforts to breed a writer.

Bibliography

1864 Immigration Act (An act to encourage immigration)— Sess. I, Chap. 246; 13 Stat. 385.— 38th Congress; July 4, 1864.

Abraham Lincoln: "Third Annual Message," December 8, 1863. Online by Gerhard Peters and John T. Woolley, The American Presidency Project. presidency.ucsb.edu/ws/?pid=29504 (accessed October 5, 2017).

"Acacia greggii, (Senegalia greggii), Catclaw Acacia." *Southwest Desert Flora*. Southwest Desert Flora, 21 November 2017, southwestdesert-flora.com/WebsiteFolders/All_Species/Fabaceae/ Acacia%20greg-gii,%20Catclaw%20Acacia.html (accessed March 12, 2019).

Agee, Philip. *Inside the Company: CIA Diary*. Bantam Books, 1975.

Bacon, David. *Illegal People: How Globalization Creates Migration and Criminalizes Immigrants*. Beacon Press, 2008.

Bailey, Rayna. *Immigration and Migration*. New York: Facts On File, 2008.

Bohme, Frederick G. et al. 1973. Population and Housing Inquiries in U.S. Decennial Censuses, 1790-1970. U.S. Bureau of the Census, Working Paper No. 39. Washington DC: U.S. Government Printing Office.

Booth, John A., et al. *Understanding Central America: Global Forces, Rebellion, and Change*. 6th ed., Westview Press, 2015.

"Border Patrol History." *U.S. Customs and Border Protection*. U.S. Department of Homeland Security, (n/d), cbp.gov/border-security/along-us-borders/history (accessed October 24, 2017).

"Cable Act of 1922." *Immigration to the United States*. immigrationtotheunitedstates.org, (n/d), immigrationtounitedstates.org/397-cable-act-of-1922.html (accessed October 10, 2017).

Calavita, Kitty. *U.S. Immigration Law and the Control of Labor: 1820-1924*. London: Academic Press, 1984.

Campbell, Duncan. "Philip Agee: The man who blew the whistle on the CIA's backing of military dictatorships." *The Guardian*. Guardian News & Media Limited, 10 January 2008, theguardian.com/news/2008/jan/10/mainsection.duncancampbell (accessed February 5, 2019).

Cantor, Guillermo. "Hieleras (Iceboxes) in the Rio Grande Valley Sector." *American Immigration Council*, AIC, December 17 2015, americanimmigrationcouncil.org/ research/hieleras-iceboxes-rio-grande-valley-sector (accessed February 13, 2018).

"CEM - Conferencia del Episcopado Mexicano." *Estudio Sobre las Casas de Migrantes Católicas*, CEM, 1 June 2017, cem.org.mx/Slider/58-ESTUDIO-SOBRE-LAS-CASAS-DE-MIGRA NTES-CAT%C3%93LICAS.html (accessed March 21, 2019).

Chomsky, Aviva. *"They Take Our Jobs!": And 20 Other Myths about Immigration*. Boston, MA: Beacon, 2007.

Chomsky, Noam. *Hopes and Prospects*. Penguin Books, 2011.

---. *Making the Future Occupations, Interventions, Empire and Resistance*. City Lights Books, 2012.

---. *Occupy*. Penguin Books, 2012.

---. *Who Rules the World?* Metropolitan Books, 2016.

Coerver, Don M., and Linda B. Hall. *Texas and the Mexican Revolution: A Study in State and National Border Policy, 1910-1920*. San Antonio, TX: Trinity UP, 1984.

Dávila, Genoveva Roldán and García, Nancy Pérez, ed. *Construyendo un modelo de atención para mujeres migrantes víctimas de violencia sexual, en México*. México, D.F.: Incide Social, 2012.

"Deferred Action for Childhood Arrivals (DACA) Data Tools." *Migration Policy Institute*, MPI, 5 December 2018, migrationpolicy.org/programs/data-hub/deferred-action-childhood-arrivals-daca-profiles (accessed January 29, 2019).

Dickinson, Eliot. *Globalization and Migration: a World in Motion*. Rowman Et Littlefield, 2017.

"ECLAC— Economic Commission for Latin America and the Caribbean." *ECLAC: At Least 2,795 Women Were Victims of Femicide in 23 Countries of Latin America and the Caribbean in 2017*, ECLAC, 15 November 2018, cepal.org/en/pressreleases/eclac-least-2795-women-were-victims-femicide-23-countries-latin-america-and-caribbean (accessed March 21, 2019).

Ettinger, Patrick W. *Imaginary Lines: Border Enforcement and the Origins of Undocumented Immigration, 1882-1930*. Austin: U of Texas, 2009.

Farthing, Linda. "The Time to Finally Stop the 'War on Drugs' Is Now." *NACLA Report on the Americas*, vol. 48, no. 4, Winter. 2006, 320-321.

Faux, Jeff. "How NAFTA Failed Mexico." *The American Prospect*, TAP, June 16 2003, prospect.org/article/how-nafta-failed-mexico. (accessed October 20, 2016)

Foley, Neil. *The White Scourge: Mexicans, Blacks, And Poor Whites in Texas Cotton Culture*. Berkeley: University of California Press, 1997. eBook Collection (EBSCOhost) (accessed November 1, 2016).

Gelatt, Julia. "More Than a DREAM (Act), Less Than a Promise." *MPI— Migration Policy Institute*, Migration Policy Institute, March 2019, migrationpolicy.org/news/more-dream-act-less-promise (accessed March 19, 2019).

Gibson, C. and Jung, Kay. "Historical Census Statistics on the Foreign-Born Population of the United States: 1850-2000." *United States Census Bureau.* U.S. Department of Commerce, February 2006, census.gov/population/www/documentation/twps0081/twps0081.html (accessed January 24, 2017).

Girardi, María Amalia, et al. *Mujeres Transmigrantes.* Org. by Oscar Arturo Castro Soto. Puebla: Universidad Iberoamericana, Centro de Estudios Sociales y Culturales Antonio de Montesinos, A. C., 2010.

Guskin, Jane, and David L. Wilson. *The Politics of Immigration: Questions and Answers.* New York: Monthly Review, 2007.

Gutman, Herbert G. *Work, Culture, and Society in Industrializing America: Essays in American Working-class and Social History.* New York: Knopf, 1976.

Handbook of Labor Statistics. Washington: Government Printing Office, 1931. Web.

Henderson, Timothy J. *A Glorious Defeat: Mexico and its war with the United States.* New York: Hill and Wand, 2008.

---. *Beyond Borders: A History of Mexican Migration to the United States.* Malden, MA: Wiley-Blackwell, 2011.

Herman, Edward S., and Chomsky, Noam. *Manufacturing consent: The Political Economy of the Mass Media.* New York: Pantheon Books, 2002.

Hondagneu-Sotelo, Pierrette, and Ernestine Avila. "'I'm Here, But I'm There': The Meanings of Latina Transnational Motherhood." Gender & Society, vol. 11, no. 5, 1997, 548-571.

International Migration Report 2002. New York, NY: UN. Department of Economic and Social Affairs, 2002.

Isacson, Adam and Meyer, Maureen. "The Alarming Rise of Migrant Deaths on U.S. Soil— And What to Do About It." *WOLA: Advocacy for Human Rights in the Americas*, Washington Office on Latin America, 24 April 2013, wola.org/analysis/the-alarming-rise-of-migrant-deaths-on-us-soil-and-what-to-do-about-it (accessed April18, 2017).

Johnson, Chalmers. *Blowback*. New York: Metropolitan Books, 2000.

Kanstroom, Dan. *Aftermath: Deportation Law and the New American Diaspora*. New York: Oxford U, 2014.

---. *Deportation Nation: Outsiders in American History*. Harvard Univ. Press, 2010.

Kelly, Lara. "Neoliberalism in Latin America." *Citizens' Press*, CP, (n/d), cpress.org/editorials/old/neoliberalism-in-latin-america (accessed May 8, 2018).

Klein, Naomi. *The Shock Doctrine: The Rise of Disaster Capitalism*. New York: Metropolitan Books/Henry Holt, 2007.

Kuhner, Gretchen. "La Violencia Contra las Mujeres Migrantes en Tránsito por México." *Revista de Derechos Humanos - Dfensor*. June 2011: 19-25.

---. "Seminario Internacional sobre Mujeres Migrantes." Instituto para las Mujeres en la Migración, A.C., *Situaciones, Discursos, y Estrategias Relacionadas con las Mujeres Migrantes Mexicanas hacia Estados Unidos y Canadá*, 2011.

Lindsay-Poland, John. "Beyond the Drug War: The Pentagon's Other Operations in Latin America." *NACLA Report on the Americas*, vol. 44, no. 3, May 2011, 8-11.

Macías-Rojas, Patrisia. *From Deportation to Prison: The Politics of Immigration Enforcement in Post-civil Rights America*. New York: New York UP, 2016.

MacLaury, Judson. "A Brief History: The U.S. Department of Labor." *U.S. Department of Labor*. United States Department of Labor, (n/d), dol.gov/general/aboutdol/history/ dolhistoxford (accessed October 26, 2017).

McWilliams, Carey. *North from Mexico: The Spanish-speaking People of the United States*. New York: Greenwood, 1968.

Mendoza, Elva F. Orozco. "Feminicide and *the Funeralization of the City*: On Thing Agency and Protest Politics in Ciudad Juárez." *Theory & Event*, vol. 20 no. 2, 2017, 351-380. *Project MUSE*, muse.jhu. edu/article/655776 (accessed March 20, 2018).

Mexico. Secretaría de Gobernación. Consejo Nacional de Población. *La Migración Femenina Mexicana a Estados Unidos. Tendencias Actuales.* Boletín de Migración Internacional. 2013. (Year I, 1).

Mexico. Secretaría de Gobernación. Consejo Nacional de Población. *Mujeres Centroamericanas en Tránsito por México con Destino a Estados Unidos.* Boletín de Migración Internacional. 2013. (Year I, 2).

Montaner, Mariliana. *Mujeres que Cruzan Fronteras.* Mexico, D.F.: Secretaría de Relaciones Exteriores de México, 2006.

"MRI's Origins." *Migrants Rights International*, MRI, (n/d), migrantsrightsinternational.org/mri-origins (accessed January 17, 2019).

Nevins, Joseph. "How US policy in Honduras set the stage for today's migration." *The Conversation*, The Conversation US, Inc., 31 October 2016, theconversation.com/how-us-policy-in-honduras-set-the-stage-for-todays-migration-65935a (accessed January 17, 2019).

Organización de los Estados Americanos. Comisión Interamericana de Derechos Humanos. *Derechos humanos de los migrantes y otras personas en el contexto de la movilidad humana en México.* Edited by the Relatoría sobre los Derechos de los Migrantes de la Comisión Interamericana de Derechos Humanos. ser. L/V/II, num. 48, 2013, 95-97.

Orrenius, Pia M., and Madeline Zavodny. *Beside the Golden Door: U.S. Immigration Reform in a New Era of Globalization.* Washington, D.C.: AEI, 2010.

Paredes, Américo, and Richard Bauman. *Folklore and Culture on the Texas-Mexican Border.* Austin, TX: CMAS, Center for Mexican American Studies, U of Texas at Austin, 1993.

Reisler, Mark. *By the Sweat of Their Brow: Mexican Immigrant Labor in the United States, 1900-1940*. Westport, CT: Greenwood, 1976.

Reiss, Suzanna. "Beyond Supply and Demand: Obama's Drug Wars in Latin America." *NACLA Report on the Americas*, vol. 43, no. 1, Jan. 2010, 27-31.

"Roosevelt Corollary to the Monroe Doctrine, 1904." *Office of the Historian*. United States Department of State, (n/d), history.state.gov/ milestones/1899-1913/roosevelt-and-monroe-doctrine   (accessed November 8, 2018).

Ryon, Sean. "Aid, and agua, along the border." *Nation Swell*, Nation-Swell, 11 July 2018, nationswell.com/water-station-mexico-border (accessed December 11, 2018).

Schoultz, Lars. *Beneath the United States: a History of U.S. Policy toward Latin America*. Harvard University, 1998.

Schwartz, Mattathias. "'Come On Down to the Rio Grande Valley. I'll Show You Around.' Would patrolling with the Border Patrol change your mind about the border?" *New York*, New York Media LLC., 6 January 2019, nymag.com/intelligencer/2019/01/border-patrol-texas-immigration.html (accessed February 26, 2019).

Soble, Ronald L. "Big Corral--End of Line for Many Aliens : Immigration: The South Texas facility houses illegal border crossers, primarily from the 'Central American Triangle.'" *Los Angeles Times*, Los Angeles Times, 26 November 1990, latimes.com/archives/la-xpm-1990-11-26-mn-3979-story.html (accessed February 26, 2019).

Spener, David. *Clandestine Crossings: Migrants and Coyotes on the Texas-Mexico Border*. Ithaca: Cornell UP, 2009.

Staudt, Kathleen and Campbell, Howard. "The Other Side of the Ciudad Juárez Femicide Story." *ReVista*, David Rockefeller Center - Harvard University, (n/d), revista.drclas.harvard.edu/ book/other-side-ciudad-ju%C3%A1rez-femicide-story (accessed May 17, 2018).

"The Cost of Immigration Enforcement and Border Security." *American Immigration Council*, American Immigration Council, 25 January 2017, americanimmigrationcouncil.org/ research/the-cost-of-immigration-enforcement-and-border-security (accessed May 15, 2018).

"The Treaty of Guadalupe Hidalgo." *National Archives*. The U.S. National Archives and Records Administration, (n/d.), archives.gov/education/lessons/guadalupe-hidalgo (accessed October 25, 2016).

Tirman, John. *Immigration and the American Backlash*. Cambridge, MA: MIT Press, 2015.

"US Army School of the Americas (USARSA/SOA)." *GlobalSecurity.org*, GlobalSecurity.org, (n/d), globalsecurity.org/military/agency/army/soa.htm (accessed November 20, 2018).

U.S. Citizenship and Immigration Services. *Immigration and Citizenship Data*. USCIS, uscis.gov/tools/reports-studies/immigration-forms-data/data-set-form-i-821d-deferred-action-childhood-arrivals (accessed September 21, 2017).

United States, Congress, Senate, United States Accountability Office, *Illegal Immigration: Border Crossing Deaths Have Doubled Since 1995; Border Patrol's Efforts to Prevent Deaths Have Not Been Fully Evaluated*. Government Printing Office, 2006.

United States, Congress. Public Law 89-732. *An Act to Adjust the Status of Cuban Refugees to That of Lawful Permanent Residents of the United States, and for Other Purposes*, 1996, pp. 1161. U.S. *U.S. Government Publishing Office*, www.govinfo.gov/content/pkg/ STATUTE-80/pdf/STATUTE-80-Pg1161.pdf

United States, Homeland Security, *FY 2019: Budget in Brief*. DHS, 2019.

United States, Homeland Security, Office of Immigration Statistics, *Population Estimates - Illegal Alien Population Residing in the United States: January 2015*. DHS Office of Immigration Statistics, 2018.

United States, U.S. Department of Labor. *Annual report of the Commissioner General of Immigration to the Secretary of Labor*, 1922. *U.S. Government Publishing Office*, https://babel.hathitrust.org/cgi/pt?id=uc1.c006010659;view=1up;seq=7 (accessed March 28, 2017).

Villegas, Rodrigo Dominguez. "Central American Migrants and 'La Bestia': The Route, Dangers, and Government Responses." *Migration Policy Institute*, MPI, 10 September 2014, migrationpolicy.org/article/central-american-migrants-and-%E2%80%9Cla-bestia%E2%80%9D-route-dangers-and-government-responses (accessed March 21, 2019).

Walshe, Sadhbh. "'Operation Endgame' and the profitable purge of legal immigrants." *The Guardian*. Guardian News & Media Limited, 11 July 2012, theguardian.com/ commentisfree/2012/jul/11/operation-endgame-purge-legal-immigrants (accessed may 10, 2018).

Wellman, Christopher and Cole, Phillip. *Debating the Ethics of Immigration: Is There a Right to Exclude?* Oxford University Press, 2011.

"Western Hemisphere Institute for Security Cooperation (WHINSEC)." *Fort Benning - U.S. Army Fort Benning and The Maneuver Center of Excellence*. U.S. Army, 10 October 2018, benning.army.mil/tenant/whinsec/History.html (accessed November 15, 2018).

Yang, Philip Q. *Post-1965 Immigration to the United States: Structural Determinants*. Westport, CT: Praeger, 1995.

Zhou, Min. *Contemporary Trends in Immigration to the United States: Gender, Labor-Market Incorporation, and Implications for Family Formation*. vol. 2, num. 2, 2003, 77-95. (Migraciones Internacionales Series).

Zinn, Howard. *A People's History of the United States*. Harper Perennial, 2015.

Zolberg, Aristide R. *A Nation by Design: Immigration Policy in the Fashioning of America*. Cambridge, MA: Harvard University Press, 2006.

Interviews

A, R. Personal Interview. 27 July 2017.

G, J. M. Personal Interview. 27 July 2017.

M, M. Personal Interview. 20 September 2017.

R, A. Personal Interview. 15 November 2017.

R, A. R. Personal Interview. 29 July 2017.

R, C. Personal Interview. 30 July 2017.

R, J. Personal Interview. 29 July 2017.

T, P. Personal Interview. 30 July 2017.

V, A. Personal Interview. 27 July 2017.

V, M. Personal Interview. 27 July 2017.

www.ingramcontent.com/pod-product-compliance
Lightning Source LLC
Chambersburg PA
CBHW030619220526

45463CB00004B/1347